T0368134

# Let Your Heart Speak

## Truth Lies Within

Jacinta Yang

**BALBOA.**PRESS
A DIVISION OF HAY HOUSE

Balboa Press books may be ordered through booksellers or by contacting:

Balboa Press
A Division of Hay House
1663 Liberty Drive
Bloomington, IN 47403
www.balboapress.com
844-682-1282

Because of the dynamic nature of the Internet, any web addresses or links contained in this book may have changed since publication and may no longer be valid. The views expressed in this work are solely those of the author and do not necessarily reflect the views of the publisher, and the publisher hereby disclaims any responsibility for them.

The author of this book does not dispense medical advice or prescribe the use of any technique as a form of treatment for physical, emotional, or medical problems without the advice of a physician, either directly or indirectly. The intent of the author is only to offer information of a general nature to help you in your quest for emotional and spiritual well-being. In the event you use any of the information in this book for yourself, which is your constitutional right, the author and the publisher assume no responsibility for your actions.

Any people depicted in stock imagery provided by Getty Images are models, and such images are being used for illustrative purposes only. Certain stock imagery © Getty Images.

Credit: Stella Graphix, Hollie@creativesolutions

Print information available on the last page.

ISBN: 979-8-7652-5445-5 (sc)
ISBN: 979-8-7652-5446-2 (hc)
ISBN: 979-8-7652-5444-8 (e)

Library of Congress Control Number: 2024915808

Balboa Press rev. date: 11/15/2024

I would like to express my heartfelt dedication to Dusty and Kevin Watson, my cherished chosen family, for their support throughout the creation of this book. Their generosity has been invaluable, and I am immensely grateful.

Dusty, the exceptionally skilled photographer and owner of Thru a Dusty Lens Photography, not only shared her remarkable photography expertise but also demonstrated her kindness by generously volunteering her time at the Free Spirit Festival, which I organized in July 2023. One notable highlight was her capture of the breathtaking image titled *Girl in Silk* during the festival's show, generously sponsored by Julie Danaylov of Cirque Revolution who is also a proud sponsor of this book. This showcased Dusty's exceptional talent and keen eye for detail.

Moreover, Dusty beautifully documented the arch I decorated for a wedding event, showcasing her versatility as a photographer. Her passion for wildlife and nature is evident in every photograph she takes, making her an extraordinary and well-rounded artist.

To Dusty and Kevin, thank you for your love and support and your contribution. This book is dedicated to you both with heartfelt gratitude.

As a dedicated volunteer at Hospice Georgina, I provide healing services to their clients. I am deeply grateful to my incredible friends and clients for supporting me with their generous donations to Hospice Georgina.

My heartfelt gratitude goes to a dear friend, Brian Darwen, who has supported me over the years personally and professionally. Knowing how much helping Hospice Georgina is dear to my heart, he has generously donated five thousand dollars annually since I joined. Join me in reaching out to others for their support in sustaining this vital cause.

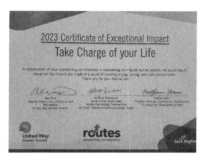

I am grateful for this certificate acknowledging my role in the Take Charge of Your Life workshop, sponsored by United Way and Routes. The images depict transformative moments, showcasing engaged participants and the workshop's palpable impact.

Inspired by the grant, I've developed additional workshops, aiming to reach a broader audience for a wider impact. This certificate celebrates the journey from inspiration to action, capturing my dedication to community empowerment.

Honoured to receive this recognition, I remain committed to making a positive difference in my community through accessible and empowering workshops.

# Acknowledgements

I extend my heartfelt gratitude to all my friends and clients whose invaluable support and encouragement have brought *Let Your Heart Speak: Truth Lies Within* to life. Your wisdom and continuous support have made this book a reality.

A special thank-you goes to those clients and friends who have generously supported the publication of this book and prefer to remain anonymous. Your financial contributions speak volumes, signifying a deep belief in the work, for which I am truly grateful. Your support means the world to me. My gratitude goes out to Chris Sanyu Lin, an experienced and valued acupuncturist at Jacinta Healing Arts, Ivan Leong, Viviane Sy, Nena Lim and my sister Agnes Yang for being the proud sponsor of this book.

A big shout-out to Krista Tucci for having supported me since the very first book I published. Her patience and generosity in everything I do are just beyond words. Krista's been there in every way possible, and I can't thank her enough. Krista, you have been a crucial part of my journey in publishing books.

Thank you to all my clients once again for trusting me to work with you on your healing journeys. You have been the motivating factor behind this book. It is our interactions, conversations, and shared experiences that provided insights and perspectives. Your stories, struggles, and triumphs have been the true inspiration breathing life into the pages of this book.

Your trust in my abilities as a writer, mentor, and healer has been humbling, and I am forever grateful for the opportunities you have given me to be a part of your journeys. Our sessions together have been a reminder of the beauty and complexity of the human experience, urging me to dive deeper into the world of emotions and the mysteries of the heart.

Thank you for being brave and sharing your feelings with me. Your openness helps me understand and care more. Those moments of sharing make this book full of understanding and kindness.

I would also like to acknowledge those who have been supportive and share your wisdom which has been a good guide in my journey.

To my friends and family, your love and encouragement have been the constant fuel pushing me forward on this writing journey. Your belief in me, even during moments of self-doubt, has been a guiding light that has helped me navigate through the challenges of this creative endeavour.

To my clients and the incredible souls who have touched my life in various ways, thank you for being the living testament to the power of our shared human experiences. May this book, *Let Your Heart Speak: Truth Lies Within*, be the guiding light to highlight the beauty within us.

*Let Your Heart Speak* is intended to help you talk openly. I share stories to help you know yourself better and have better relationships. I share what I've learned from my life and what I've seen. My hope is for you to speak honestly and trust in your relationships.

I share my insights to help you communicate truthfully from your heart. It's about having a kind and open space for your feelings.

Imagine a world where everyone is honest and open, where problems get resolved peacefully, and where people are kind. This book shares how we can achieve mutual respect by adopting love and compassion.

I hope it changes how you relate to others. Communicating

honestly can bring us closer and allow us to be kinder. Being open and honest is hard, but it helps us connect for real. Be truthful but kind to each other. The purpose of this book is to help you grow by expressing yourself for stronger and deeper relationships. Let's spread love and kindness by speaking from our hearts. We can make the world a better place. That's the essence of what I wanted to share.

# Contents

# Chapter 1

## The Voice Within

## 1. The Power of Intuition

WHAT IS INTUITION? YOU MAY ALREADY HAVE AN UNDERSTANDING of what intuition is. It is an inner knowing of something without really knowing how you know what you know. It's like an inner voice that tells us the right direction to take when we are faced with some difficult choices. Intuition is that voice that is beyond conscious awareness, making it sometimes hard to rationalize or explain.

Have you ever found yourself in a situation in which you were going somewhere and you felt a gut feeling you couldn't exactly explain but that made it seem as if a voice in your head were telling you to turn around? If so, that was your intuition talking to you, trying to protect you from impending harm. Intuition can also guide you in less drastic situations as well, such as determining which job to choose or who may not be a good potential partner.

Some think that people with psychic gifts tend to possess such power. This is not necessarily true. Anyone can develop intuition. It doesn't defy logic or reason. Logic and intuition can complement each other by allowing the weighing of pros and cons and making decisions based on them. Intuition helps us to reach into our subconscious minds to help us make decisions without any logical explanation or judgement.

I suggest you combine logic and intuition when making your decisions. I personally prefer to use logic when I am making any decision because I am a very logical person, but because I am intuitive I also like to use my intuition to confirm the decisions I make. I like the additional guidance from my intuition that helps me feel at ease with the decisions. I like to combine my logic and my intuition when I am making any decisions, because I feel and have noticed that I do not regret any decisions made when I do that.

I have always been a very logical person, as you know if you have read my book *Take Charge: Reclaim Your Life and Be Your True Self.* Over the years, Logic has on many occasions interfered with my gifts which I have talked about in my book *My Spiritual Journey: Life as an Empath.*

Since I was very attuned to my intuition, I did follow them and found it to be very helpful. I was always very attuned to my body's reactions to these intuitive hits and have been able to sense and know that I should follow them.

I consider intuition as guidance from our guardian angels or spirit guides; that is why I feel protected and know that I should trust my instincts or intuition.

While intuition may seem magical, there's a scientific basis behind this phenomenon. Our brains have the capability to process large amounts of information even beyond our imaginations because they are very complex. Our subconscious minds pick up on certain patterns and subtle cues that we may not remember consciously. As INFJ personality types, we are highly intuitive.

For example, when we meet someone for the first time, we may sense something from his or her body language, how the person speaks, and the expressions on his or her face, and we react according to how we feel from such encounters or the impressions we get from them. This provides us with an initial impression that guides our interaction. You may have experienced having an instant like or dislike for someone when meeting him or her for the first time. This is how intuition sometimes helps us.

INFJ personality types are known to be able to predict outcomes by recognizing patterns. Researchers argue that intuition stems from the brain's ability to detect and analyse patterns by accumulating knowledge over a period of time and forming connections in our neurons to help us recognize similar patterns and predict outcomes without being consciously aware of recalling the details.

Research done on empaths has found that their neurons patterns are different to those of most people. That is why we empaths, or highly sensitive people (HSPs), can sense and feel more than the average population. Our brains are wired differently. I trust my intuition, but due to my logical nature, I seek confirmation in certain situations, especially when it involves others. I avoid making assumptions based solely on intuition and prefer certainty when making decisions.

Trusting your intuition can be very challenging, especially when the world puts emphasis on rationality and concrete evidence. However, learning to rely on your gut feeling can lead to more authentic and fulfilling experiences.

I feel that the human body is like a weather forecaster that prompts us about what is happening within us. Pay attention to your intuition, your emotions, and your gut feeling; listen to how your body reacts. When we feel comfortable, it indicates that we're okay and things are fine, whereas a sense of discomfort might suggest a need for caution.

Try remembering a time when your intuition guided you through a past experience, and think about how helpful it was. I am sure there were times when you ignored your intuition or gut feeling only to regret it later. Understanding how your intuition has been helpful to you in the past helps you to have trust in your intuition in the future.

I would suggest you be aware of what you feel by allowing yourself to be present in the moment and be aware of how your day is going. You will then be able to feel and know the subtle changes that you will experience throughout the day. This helps you to be more in tune with your thoughts and emotions. This self-awareness helps you to develop your intuition.

Be open to uncertainty because you can experience intuition at any moment or in any situation. When you are open to listening to your gut feelings or intuition, it may not make logical sense, and that is okay. When your intuition helps you with some decisions, don't be afraid to consider other information to confirm your feelings. When I say you should trust your intuition, that doesn't mean you must not analyse the situation thoroughly. Intuition can help us in both life-changing situations and menial decisions.

Intuition helps us gauge others' intentions and emotions, allowing us to connect with people authentically. We might feel drawn to certain individuals or repelled by others based on our intuitive perceptions.

There are times when we can be easily fooled. This includes me, despite my being quite in tune. There are times when your intuition may tell you or warn you about a person who is portraying himself or herself as someone with good intentions or a seemingly caring and generous person.

I tend to give people the benefit of the doubt in such circumstances, which means that I may ignore an intuitive nudge. Although I do keep note of these nudges when I am able to confirm them, I occasionally choose to ignore them. This practice is handy because it prevents me from feeling surprised by my realization later on.

Intuition plays a huge role in parenting. It helps us to understand a child's needs as well as make tough decisions on how to guide children as they are relying on us parents to help and teach them. Our bodies also will let us know about our own health and well-being through our intuition. It is that inner voice that will tell us to seek out medical advice and that helps us know in advance that we have a health issue.

From understanding a child's needs to making tough choices, parents often rely on their intuition to guide them. I teach my students in my intuitive workshop to be in tune with their bodies, as the body is a barometer for intuitive nudges. When we are keenly aware of our bodies, we will be able to know or feel when we are getting the intuitive hits.

Intuition is a powerful tool that complements our logical thinking, guiding us through life's challenges. By learning to trust our gut feeling, we can tap into a wealth of unconscious knowledge and make more informed decisions. Intuition is not a mystical force, but rather a natural aspect of our human cognition, honed through experiences and learning. Be open to your intuition and you may find yourself navigating life's journey with new-found clarity and confidence.

## 2. Your Inner Voice

I would like to share something close to my heart—listening to your inner voice, also known as intuition—that little voice inside you that nudges you in certain directions.

I will be honest with you; I used to dismiss my intuition a lot because I'm a logical person, and I often find logical reasons or impractical reasons to shrug it away. But guess what? Ignoring my intuition often led me to regret and caused me to wish I had listened to it. But then I realized our inner voice is like a secret superpower! It's this inner voice that can help us to make better choices, find our true selves, and have more fulfilling lives.

It's hard to hear that inner voice when we are too busy, engrossed in our daily lives, and feeling overwhelmed. We tend to cater to the expectations of others, our own doubts, and the constant rush of life. Trust me, it's worth the effort to tune in.

I am happy to share with you what I have experienced in my personal journey. First off, it's okay to be a little scared of trusting your intuition. I was reluctant because of my logical mindset. We are often concerned about what others may think or say. It's *your* life, and you get to live it as authentically as you want. Listening to your inner voice means being true to yourself, and that's pretty powerful!

Society has a tendency to rely on logical thinking and solid evidence. It's all about the numbers; data; and cold, hard facts. I am sure those are essential in many situations. But intuition complements logic! It's like having a secret ingredient that adds to your decision-making.

How do we nurture that connection with our intuition? It starts with setting aside some time for stillness and quiet. I know life can be crazy busy, but trust me, finding time for yourself is rewarding. You can meditate, go for a walk in nature, or just sit alone with your thoughts.

Mindfulness is another great tool! Being present in the moment helps you notice those subtle nudges from your intuition. And don't forget to write down your thoughts and feelings in a journal. Journaling is a very important exercise. It's like keeping a secret diary with your inner wisdom, and it can help you detect patterns and gain insights.

Speaking of insights, remember those times when your intuition led you in the right direction? Celebrate those moments! Pat yourself on the back and say, "Way to go, inner voice!" Building trust in your intuition takes time, but celebrating your wins makes it easier. I always tell my clients to reward themselves with gold stars for all their accomplishments, no matter how minor they may be.

It's normal to have moments when we doubt ourselves or when we've ignored our intuition in the past. I have done that on many occasions and found that wasn't a very smart move. But let's not be hard on ourselves about it. Instead, let's see those times as opportunities to learn and grow. Every experience, whether it is good or bad, helps us become more in tune with our inner voices.

Surrounding yourself with supportive people can make a world of difference! Seek out friends and loved ones who encourage you to trust your intuition and embrace your true self. It's like having your own support system, and it helps boost your confidence.

In my earlier years, I did not know many people who were spiritual or who even remotely understood anything about the gifts I was born with. I had a very sheltered life; my parents did not make a big deal about it. I was just me as I am with my gifts; it was a normal part of me. It was when I was away from my family that I realized I was different. I am more attuned to my inner voice than I realized.

So, in a nutshell, listening to your inner voice is like unlocking your superpower. It leads to better decisions, less stress, and a more authentic life. Sure, it might take some practice, but it is worth it! Life becomes clearer, and you'll feel more content and at peace with yourself. Through the Healing Journey Program, my clients have learned to pay attention to the subtle nudges they get from intuition, and through practice they have adopted the skills and have achieved clarity and peace for themselves.

Take a moment, close your eyes, take a deep breath, and listen to that gentle whisper inside you. Your intuition is waiting to guide you towards a brighter, happier future. Accept it, trust it, and let it lead the way!

## 3. Wisdom of Your Heart

Allow some quiet time for yourself, in a quiet room in your home or a peaceful spot in the garden or a park, and breathe. Consider your heart as a dear friend, a tiny wise sage living within you.

Close your eyes and connect with that feeling. Your heart speaks through feelings, nudges, and those gut instincts you often feel.

Life can get hectic and loud, and we often forget to listen to our hearts amidst all the noise of our daily lives. But when we take a moment to listen, to really tune in, we open up the treasure chest of our hearts, revealing all that wonderful wisdom inside. This isn't easy, because our minds have the tendency to worry and fear, making it hard to hear the soft whispers of our hearts. However, it's worth tuning in and listening.

Tune in to those subtle sensations and emotions; they're the language of your heart. I tell my clients and students to pay attention to all those minute subtle sensations they feel so that they may become truly attuned. Your heart might surprise you with its wisdom! It might remind you of dreams and passions you've set aside. Your heart can guide you through those tough decisions you've been dealing with. It may also simply fill you with a sense of peace, assuring you that everything will be okay.

By listening to your heart, you connect yourself to something greater than yourself which is special and wonderful. Some call it the universe; others call it the higher self or divine guidance. It's like being part of something beautiful and great, and your heart is leading the way.

Just like any relationship, it requires nurturing and attention on an ongoing basis. Make it a habit to check in with your heart regularly. Try to determine how it feels, what it needs, and what it wants to share with you.

When you are living a life aligned with your heart's wisdom, life becomes more meaningful and fulfilling. You find yourself making choices that resonate with your soul, attracting experiences and people that uplift you. Trusting more makes this alignment easier

Life isn't all rainbows and butterflies. I posed the question to my workshop participants, "Who agrees with the phrase 'life is not a bed of roses'?" Everyone raised a hand, and all were surprised when I said I didn't agree with that phrase. I don't agree with it because roses come with thorns, and life is and always will be filled with some sorts of challenges, and it is up to us how we handle them. That's when leaning into your heart's wisdom becomes even more crucial.

Life is often filled with challenges; therefore, it won't always be smooth sailing—and that's okay. When you face difficult times, turn to your heart's wisdom. Remember the guidance it's given you before. Trust in yourself that you have the strength and wisdom to get through anything life throws your way. It's like having a sturdy anchor to hold on to amidst the stormy waters. It is our inner wisdom that guides us through the difficult times.

I encourage you to embrace the wisdom of your heart. Trust in its guidance even when it feels scary or uncertain. Listen to its whispers and follow its lead. Releasing the wisdom of your heart is like setting free a beautiful bird; it soars high and leads you to places you never imagined possible.

You have everything you need inside you: wisdom, strength, and love. It's all there, waiting for you to open up the treasure chest and let it shine. Allow your heart to be your guide, and watch how your life unfolds. You all can do this if you allow yourself.

## 4. Overcoming Doubt and Fear

I think fear is the number-one problem that tends to affect everyone in the world regularly. Even those who are strong on a mental or emotional level face fear from time to time. Everyone I know assumes I am fearless, but that is far from the truth. I feel fear just like everyone else. I do not let fear paralyze me. I feel it, acknowledge it, and find a solution to overcome it.

Making choices can be challenging. I encourage my clients to overcome fear, and I guide them on how to take steps to deal with the fear. The purpose of this book is to help you conquer those doubts and fears, and to help you to be confident in making decisions.

How would you define doubts? They can be like little voices in our minds, whispering, "What if things go wrong? What if I fail?" This is the most common fear among the clients I mentor. However, it's important to remember that doubts are just thoughts and not reality. Doubts are generally fuelled by fear and irrational thoughts.

I hear all the time from clients about how they fear things going wrong or not going the way they want things to go, which tends to paralyze them and prevent them from making a decision.

One way to handle doubts is to challenge them. When a doubt arises, ask yourself, "Are there any facts to support this?" More often than not, you'll find there's no real reason for those negative thoughts. It is best to have a positive mindset and reprogram your thoughts and doubts into positive questions, such as "What if I succeed beyond what I imagine?" and to visualize in your mind a positive outcome. This frame of mind helps to boost your confidence.

Fear seems to have a paralyzing effect on people who tend to stop themselves from taking steps in making any decision for fear they might make the wrong one.

Anyone can overcome fear by taking the first step and moving forward.

Start by acknowledging fear and facing it head-on. It's natural to feel scared, as we're all human. However, don't allow fear to prevent you from doing anything. Recognize it, take a deep breath, and tell yourself, "I can do this. I am strong and capable." If it happens to be the wrong decision, you can always learn from it and try again.

Trying to imagine a positive outcome can also help you overcome fear. Close your eyes and imagine succeeding in making that decision. Picture the joy and satisfaction you'll feel.

Visualizing success can calm those butterflies of fear in your stomach.

When you don't have enough information about your choices in making a decision, doubts and fears have a way of creeping into your thoughts. It's like walking into a dark space without a flashlight to show you the way. To overcome this, you can shed light on what you need to shed light on. Fears often stem from the unknown—from not knowing what to expect or what lies ahead.

Take time to gather all necessary information that is relevant to making an informed choice. Research, seek advice from trusted friends or experts, or create a list of pros and cons. Having the information you need can boost your confidence and clarity. Taking baby steps is another way to fight fear. Attempt to deal with each challenge in a smaller, manageable way. It is also important to celebrate each small step.

Be open to seeking advice from trusted friends or experts, or create a list of pros and cons. Doing research and gathering relevant information to help you make informed decisions, and having the right information, can boost your confidence and clarity.

It is okay that we won't always know everything. No one does. Making decisions involves some level of uncertainty. It is a natural part of life. Accept the uncertainty with open arms and trust yourself to handle whatever comes your way. Be willing to take risks. The results can be rewarding. If not, then you jot it down to experience, which oftentimes is helpful.

Intuition is that gut feeling, an inner knowing, that nudges us in a particular direction. Trust in your intuition; it's a powerful tool. When facing doubts and fears, take a moment to listen to your intuition. Tune in to how your body feels when considering each option. You will know which choice to make if you pay attention to the subtle sensations that you feel, such as feeling tense or relaxed.

Don't ignore those gut feelings; they are valuable guides.

Your intuition is like your own personal guide, directing you in the direction that feels right for you. Don't worry about making mistakes; doing so is all right because it is part of life and being human, and it's natural to make mistakes from time to time; that is how we learn and grow.

Be kind and gentle with yourself if things don't turn out as you hoped. Don't worry, but rather consider them as learning experiences, not mistakes or failures. I trust my intuition by sensing what my body tells me. If it feels right and comfortable, it generally is the way to go. If I feel unease and discomfort in my body, then I know it is best to avoid what lies ahead.

Reflect on what went well and what you could do differently next time. Whatever decisions we make, whether they lead to success or not, they are opportunities to grow and evolve. Embrace the journey! Remember: you don't have to make decisions all alone. Reach out to your support system of friends, family, and mentors; they're there to help and offer guidance.

Talking to someone you trust about your doubts and fears can be very helpful. It's like sharing the weight, so you are not carrying the burden all by yourself making it feel lighter and more manageable.

Overcoming doubt and fear in decision-making is a journey in itself. Don't worry about being perfect, but more importantly be brave enough to take that step and do something about it even when you are not sure of the outcome. It takes time and practise to learn to have faith in trust in your inner voice.

Learn to trust yourself, embrace your intuition, gather information, and seek support when you need it. It is not a weakness to seek support. It shows you have the courage to seek advice and support. Most importantly, be kind to yourself along the way. Be brave and go ahead; take risks and make decisions with confidence, listen to that voice inside you, and face whatever fears or challenges that may be ahead of you. Be proud of yourself for making that decision, no matter what the outcome is.

# 5. Intuition in a Logical World

We tend to trust facts and numbers to make decisions because we feel it is the most reliable way to do so. Most people ignore the inner feelings that guide us, because people rely on logic.

I admit I have been guilty of that myself. Even though I have a gift of strong intuition, I used to shrug it off because I wanted to make sense of everything, and intuition is something you cannot make sense of. Over time I learned how valuable intuition is for us in our daily lives.

Our intuition is like a special gift we have inside us, waiting to be acknowledged. It's that strong feeling that something is right or wrong even when we don't have clear proof. Sometimes we might ignore it, thinking it's just our imagination. I know I used to think I had a pretty wild imagination when I used to have the inner guidance or that intuitive hit.

But I soon learned how helpful it is. I then decided to follow my guidance and see what came of it, and it has helped me in so many areas of my life. In time I started to trust in what I was feeling and sensing, and soon it became a very significant part of my life I learned how helpful it has been for me and how I can follow its guidance to help others.

So how do we listen to our intuition when we live in a logical world? First, we need to know and accept that it exists and trust it. It's not about putting logic aside or ignoring it, but rather combining the two to help us make decisions that are right for us. Even though I'm usually a very logical person, I often follow my intuition without realizing it.

One way to listen to our intuition is to take some quiet time to think. In our busy lives, we often rush through everything, trying to beat time. But if we slow down, breathe, and really pay attention, we can hear what our intuition is telling us.

I rarely make quick decisions. I like to think about all the options before I even consider making a decision. Sometimes

I even imagine making a wrong choice just to get it out of my system, especially when someone has proven to be untrustworthy.

Another way to listen to our intuition is to pay attention to our feelings. Our feelings use the same language our intuition uses. When you have to decide something, notice how you feel about each option. Do you feel comfortable or uneasy or dreadful? I tend to feel dread when something does not feel right. Trust, those feelings. They're like signals from your intuition showing you the right way.

We also need to trust ourselves when we listen to our intuition. Sometimes doubts and the things others say can be very confusing and cause you to feel stuck. But do we have the ability to know what is right for us when we draw experiences from the past and learn? In the past, I often used logic to go against my intuition because my intuition didn't seem logical. But later on I realized there were good reasons to avoid certain situations.

Also, it's important to be okay with not knowing everything when we trust our intuition. It may not always come with a clear plan. We have to trust the process, even when we're not sure what will happen. I have learned that we are guided on a need-to-know basis so we are not overwhelmed. This openness to uncertainty guides us towards new opportunities and growth.

We tend to pack our days with lots of to-do lists, and we are always in a hurry, which causes a lot of noise that drowns out our intuition. But if we allow quiet time for ourselves, time to write in a journal or meditate if we so choose to, we can hear our intuition much better. Over time, with enough practice, you will be able to know when your intuition is communicating with you.

I have been very in tune with my inner guidance from a very young age—so much so that it is a part of me. I can feel and sense immediately that no matter how busy I am, I am tapped in. I do not necessarily require quiet moments to receive guidance. I am sure you, too, can achieve this once you understand the subtle indication or sensation you feel and can decipher it when the intuition presents itself.

Our friends, elders, and mentors we feel we can trust can be a good source of advice based on their own experiences. It is good to reach out to them sometimes for a sounding board. It is good to have people around us who support and respect our intuition, which I think is really helpful.

Using our intuition doesn't mean we have to ignore our logic. It means it is better to use both our logic and our feelings to make choices that are beneficial and helpful for us. Logic helps us to plan, and intuition gives us a deeper understanding.

Listening to our intuition boosts our creativity and helps us solve problems. We open ourselves up to new possibilities with the help of our intuition. When we trust it, it lets us see beyond the surface to go within our inner wisdom.

People often say we should ignore our feelings and use only our heads, but trusting our intuition is very powerful and empowering. I feel that nowadays more and more people are learning to be more open and are more accepting of what is not the norm. It's a way of saying we believe in ourselves and value our inner wisdom. People are learning to trust in the universe.

Intuition is something we all have inside us. If we recognize it and nurture it, we can make choices that are truer to ourselves and bring us more happiness. Everyone can learn and develop his or her intuition to help improve his or her daily life. I have witnessed amongst my clients that when they learn how to tap into their intuition through the workshops I teach, they find that they can go with the flow much easier and that they experience less anxiety because they are no longer fearful of what could go wrong.

When we learn to trust our intuition, we learn to trust the process of life. We become aware that not every decision will lead us to success or failure, but it's a process to help us in our personal growth.

Being open to our intuition also means being open to

15

accepting change. As we learn and grow from our experiences, our intuition may guide us in different directions, which may lead us to fulfilling lives. Being flexible and open to change allows us to follow the path that aligns with our values and who we are.

Being present in the moment and being mindful of our daily lives can help deepen our connection with our intuition. Doing these things also helps create stronger bonds in our relationships with our loved ones. Being present and mindful means being aware, which allows us to tune in to our inner guidance and wisdom.

When we trust our intuition, we will not really need outside validation from others. However, seeking advice is always helpful in aiding you to determine what feels right for you. We learn to be more self-reliant and confident in our choices, knowing that we are following our inner guidance and our authentic self. We are able to handle problems that we go through when we are not able to reach our friends or family for support.

Trusting our intuition also means having the courage to make choices that may not be acceptable to others or in line with societal and cultural norms. I had to do so because I felt I needed to do what was right for me. It's about being true to ourselves, even if it means going against what is acceptable to our own cultures of belief.

Our intuition can be very helpful in weeding out relationships as well. It can help us recognize when someone is genuine and when it's time to let go of toxic relationships that are not good for our mental well-being. I found that by trusting my intuition, I can read people fairly accurately, although I may misread some people who have a very strong mask on.

What you need to know is that Intuition is not about predicting the future or having psychic abilities. It is about listening to your inner voice, which often feels like a subtle knowing, which many people may shrug off as a strange imagination when they are not aware of how intuition works and why they are sensing and feeling something. I know I was one of them. I used to say to myself, "Oh my, do I ever have such a weird imagination," and I would often wonder why I had such imaginations. It is about listening to the inner wisdom that helps us in making choices that are aligned with our values.

It is a skill that everyone can develop. Intuition requires practice and patience. It may not always be clear or straightforward, but with time and effort, you, too, can tap into your intuition. You will discover that when you allow yourself to listen to the inner voice, you will be able to recognize the subtle nudge you get from your intuition and let it help you in your daily life.

You will soon recognize the power of your intuition while you are making any decisions. You will also notice that it helps you to find the balance between inner wisdom and rationality in our logical world. By paying attention to your emotions in the safe place that you create for reflection, you will gain insights, develop trust, and accept uncertainty, especially when you surround yourself with supportive friends and family and practise together by tuning out the external distractions.

By trusting your intuition, you will find that you have improved your problem-solving skills and will feel more creative and confident. Therefore, the choices you make will align with you and your values.

When we take all of that into consideration, it is clear that intuition is indeed a gift available to all of us. By nurturing its growth and letting go of the need for perfection, we can make more fulfilling decisions.

## 6. Strengthening Your Intuition

**Intuition has been very important and helpful in my life's journey, consistently guiding me well. This is a skill that everyone can learn to develop, and it offers great benefits to those willing to embrace it.**

A client posed a question to me: "How do you know when you get an inner guidance?" I explained to her how I feel or sense it when it happens, and I suggested she pay attention to subtle nudges or thoughts that come to mind. I also explained how our logical minds may try to talk us out of it. I advised her to take the chance and listen to it and see what the outcome is.

She felt the intuitive nudge but was not sure, but she remembered what I said about it—to just go with it and see what the outcome would be. She was amazed by the outcome, which she found unbelievable because logically it would not have been possible. She soon learned to trust her intuition or the guidance she received. I started teaching it to my clients who were doing their healing journeys with me.

Now I am teaching workshops on tapping into intuition. I would like to share with you some tips on how you, too, can develop your intuition, if you are just getting into it or would like to understand more about it. First of all, when we talk about inner wisdom or inner guidance, I will speak for myself. To me that basically means we have our own guardian angel, which some may call a spirit guide. I believe we all have our own angel or guide that is always with us to help us.

We get so busy with everyday life events that we tend to concentrate on dealing with, preventing us from hearing the guidance that we are receiving. In the rush and noise of the day-to-day chatter, our logical minds step in and shrug that guidance away. I know this for a fact because I have experienced it on many occasions. But since I do tend to pay attention to my thoughts and actions I realized that when I ignored the voice in my head, I later learned that I should have listened to it

I decided to try and listen to the voice even though it did not make logical sense, and I soon found that doing so was a great help. Gradually I learned to trust that inner voice in my head. The more you tune in and listen and go with it, the easier it becomes.

Many people may say you need to have quiet time alone to

meditate and get in touch with yourself. Blah, blah, blah! What I would suggest to you is not to worry too much about that. I don't agree entirely with that, because I did not do that, nor do I sit down quietly in a lotus position to meditate.

I am too active to meditate in the traditional ways most people talk about. I can be in a meditative state without sitting in a lotus position. The important thing to know is that if you can shut out the world and go within even though there are plenty of distractions around you, that is fine. The point of quiet meditation is quieting the mind chatter and going deep within you to get into a peaceful and calm state. I can and I do, and if I do find I am having difficulty tuning out the noise and distraction, then I will go and find myself a quiet space.

What I am trying to impart to you is that you should do what works for you as long as you can tune out the outside noise to get to your calm space.

You may also have heard "So find a quiet space because intuition loves a calm and peaceful environment, a spot where you can sit comfortably and relax. Take a few deep breaths, letting go of any tension or worries." Many people tell me they feel they cannot meditate because they cannot sit still, so they feel discouraged from meditating.

I assure them they can meditate in whatever way works for them, as it's not about sitting still but rather about stilling or quietening the mind's chatter and bringing oneself to a state of peace and quiet. If you are just getting started on this journey to tap into your intuition, remember that you can do so by being acutely aware of yourself, how you feel, and what you feel. That will be your main guide.

I am at a point in my life where I feel I am usually in a state of calm. It does not matter what is going on around me. People often comment to me that they feel calm around me or that my presence is very calming.

Some of you may find that meditation is a great way to

strengthen your intuition. That is great, and for those of you who may feel you cannot meditate, don't fret; find your method to achieve your goal. Whatever method works for you is fine. Some people find that doing repetitive chores helps them to achieve peacefulness and calmness. Being engrossed in creative activities is another method to tune in as well.

A great way to tap into your intuition is through creative activities. Being creative allows you to delve into your subconscious mind, where intuition is. I am always engaging in creative activities, and that is what helps me to tap in. There are times when I feel that taking a walk in nature or going for a hike is also helpful. I have found that walking through a labyrinth is a very effective way to tap into my inner guidance. It is truly amazing.

You may want to try different things to know what works best for you and own that method. When you do, you can start tuning in to your inner voice. Do not judge or overthink it; just listen and pay attention, allow it to flow, and pay attention to your thoughts and sensations that you feel. Soon you will be able to connect the various sensations you feel when your inner voice is talking to you, and that will help you recognize when you are getting your intuitive guidance, which will help you to strengthen your intuition.

Be consciously aware of how your body reacts to different situations. It will give you a telltale sign when something is off or when something upcoming is positive. I had a friend who wanted to know something that she was hoping for so badly and came to me for a reading.

I do not like to give anyone false hope about something significantly important that he or she has been waiting on for a long time, leading him or her to the brink of disappointment. But amazingly, my body reacted to those questions that she needed answered. I had a big smile on my face, and I felt sheer happiness.

To tell you the truth, I wanted to hold on to that feeling

forever if I could. I said to her, "Since I do not want to give you false hope, all I can do is express the sheer joy I am feeling." Two weeks later, she got positive news. This was an answer she had waited ten years for, and she was feeling the sheer joy I felt when she came to me about what she wanted to know.

I trust the very first answer that comes to me. When you ask yourself a question, your intuition often gives you an immediate response, and that is the response you want to listen to. However, our logical minds often explain these initial responses away with logical thinking and the like. Trust that first instinctual answer before your logical mind takes over with some explanation. When it comes to instinct, the first instinctual answer will arrive so fast that your logical mind should not have time to process it.

Pay attention to your dreams. Dreams are a window into your subconscious mind and can reveal valuable insights. Keep a dream journal next to your bed, and jot down any dreams or intuitive messages you recall upon waking. Some people find keeping a dream journal helpful; however, it's something I never felt drawn to do. I notice that my entire body and mind respond to intuition naturally. It surprises many of my clients how I trust my intuition strongly.

Practise gratitude regularly. Expressing gratitude opens up your heart and increases your connection with your intuition. When you're in a state of gratitude, you become more receptive to intuitive guidance. I find this to be so true for myself.

Be open to receiving signs and synchronicities from the universe. Intuitive messages can come in various forms, such as repeating numbers, symbols, or chance encounters. Stay open to and aware of these signs; they may be meaningful messages for you.

Practise intuition games and exercises with a friend or partner, such as guessing what colour the other person is thinking of or tuning in to each other's feelings without speaking. This can be a fun and playful way to strengthen your intuitional abilities together. I give exercises to my mentees to practise telepathic connection, which is somewhat connected to intuition.

They get so excited when they get confirmation of their ability to send telepathic messages. Some are successful in their initial attempts, while others needed to be more focused in their attempts. Having fun developing your intuition is a beautiful and exciting journey of self-discovery. Enjoy the process, embrace the mysteries, and trust that your intuition will guide you to greater clarity and wisdom. It is truly a powerful skill and is worthwhile to develop.

# Chapter 2

## The Courage to Be Authentic

### 1. Embracing Your True Self

Do you feel that you are going about your life trying to meet everyone's expectations and taking care of everyone else's needs before your own? There may be times when you feel you don't even exist. Embracing your true self is about being aware of yourself; acknowledging your existence; and realizing that, like everyone else, you, too, matter. It is about diving in, going within, and allowing yourself to be who you are and who you want to be rather than who others want you to be.

When you go within and learn to be aware of who you are, you soon learn to recognize your own worth. The first step in embracing your true self is acknowledging your own worth as a person. In the Healing Journey Program, the first exercise I get clients to do is make a list of what they like and dislike about themselves. Once they can identify those things, then I guide them to accept their likes and dislikes so they can embrace who they are.

I help guide them on how to convert the dislikes as part of their strengths or to use those very traits to help them become better versions of themselves. For example, a client of mine listed overthinking as one of her dislikes. I helped her to use this very trait in a beneficial way in decision-making situations and to avoid the overthinking that was causing her anxiety.

Remember: you are unique. You have your own experiences and possess your own sets of strengths and weaknesses. Self-acceptance is all about accepting everything about yourself—all your gifts, strengths, and what you consider to be your flaws or weaknesses. You don't need validation from anyone else.

When you feel you need validation from an outside source, ask yourself, "What is it about me that I am not accepting? Why do I feel I need validation from other people?" When you ask these questions, you are on the road to self-discovery. This propels you to dive within yourself to learn more about yourself.

Tell yourself you are perfect as you are with all your imperfections. We all know no one in the world is perfect. You being just as you are makes you special, if you feel there is something you do not like, you accept it and learn to make changes and grow. For example, if you feel that you are always so fearful and you do not like this about yourself, and you know that being fearful does not help you, it would be best to overcome this fear. So, basically, you acknowledge and accept the fact that you are indeed fearful, and you find ways to overcome this. You are special. Acceptance of yourself, including your weaknesses, allows you to grow and improve without putting unrealistic burdens and expectations on yourself.

Why do you think it is important for you to accept you as you are? When you are aware of yourself, you learn to grow in the process, and you start to realize your own value and your self-worth, you feel more confident in yourself and are not afraid to show your true self to the world. Being authentic and transparent starts from within. When you are aware of your worth, you won't be affected by the opinions of others. You will not be bothered by what they think of you, because you will already be aware of who you are and will be comfortable with it. You won't feel the need to compare yourself with others, because you are on your own journey and you have your own unique path.

What I have noticed is that many people that I know and have encountered show images of themselves on social media which are very different to their true selves. Although some people have integrity, are no different in real life as well as on social media. When you remove the pressure of comparing yourself with others, you are giving yourself the time to explore your interests and passions that bring you joy and contentment. You feel a sense of freedom because you are not conforming to others.

Do what you enjoy doing that will make you feel alive, whatever it may be. It could be spending time in nature, hiking, walking, dancing, painting, or even simply listening to music or reading. When you enjoy what you do, you experience a sense of purpose or satisfaction. That is why it's been said, "If you choose a job doing what you love, you will not work a day in your life." That is an amazing feeling,

To be authentic, we need to be transparent and be willing to be vulnerable. Be honest about your thoughts and feelings even when you may not feel comfortable for fear of being judged or disliked. Openness and willingness to be vulnerable allows you to build genuine relationships with others, which encourages you to be in a supportive environment where you won't feel judged.

You will learn, through experience, who is deserving of your trust and deserves to see your most vulnerable side. This is one of the ways you grow and learn who you are or what type of people you would like to have in your circle of friends. It is also a way to weed out people who are toxic and do not align with you. You develop friendships with people who share mutual understanding and are good for your emotional well-being.

It takes courage to be your true self, so you should feel proud and pat yourself on the back for taking the steps to learn to grow, going within to bring out your inner beauty, practising being vulnerable and transparent, and being your true self by willingly going through the process of being kind to yourself and discovering your unique self.

## 2. Free from Societal Expectations

No matter which part of the world or which culture you are from, the society you live in has an influence on how you live. Invisible societal rules seem to have a hold over everyone with expectations regarding how we should live. In some cultures, especially Eastern cultures, these rules seem to have a very strong influence. They can be very suffocating because they seem to dictate which careers we are to follow and whom we should love or marry. I am from a culture in which parents arrange marriages for their children.

This is something that ruled the formative years of my life, which I have written about in my first book, *Take Charge: Reclaim Your Life and Be Your True Self.* In this book I talk about how I broke free from these chains and lived life on my own terms, in hopes that you, too, can learn to do the same. This book is intended to inspire and motivate you to have the courage to break free from societal expectations and still be your kind, loving, and compassionate self.

There are many societal and cultural expectations that are so ingrained in our minds that we may not even question them. I can relate to this, because in my culture, similarly to other Asian cultures, marriages are arranged, and parents have full control of their children's lives (or so I thought). I lived the life that was expected of me by my parents. I registered for a bachelor of commerce degree despite my interest being in the arts, meeting my mother's expectations. However, I do not regret it, as all educations are valuable.

There are some people that are quite content to live the life that is expected in their cultures. That is totally fine. However, for someone like me, who is not a follower and has a mind of his or her own, that person will feel such cultures to be very restrictive. We are unique in our own ways, with different dreams, passions, and aspirations. Therefore, we need to have the freedom to be who we are and not be restricted to conform to the expectations of society or culture.

Ask yourself, "Is this what I really want? Is this what society expects of me? Does this align with my true self?" I asked myself this and felt I was not living the life that I wanted. I was married to a man who liked to control my life and did not allow me room to grow into the person I wished to be. It took courage and self-awareness and self-acceptance on my part to break free from that life.

It takes self-awareness and determination to break free, and it requires courage on our part to do so. These are our lives, and we must have the freedom to choose how we want to live and what we want to do with our own lives. That is why it is so important for us to be honest with ourselves and understand who we truly are and what our values are.

Breaking away from my controlled life was not easy, nor was it smooth sailing. I had to stay focused on what I needed to do for myself. Most of all, I had to ignore the inner and outer chatter. The inner chatter is the chatter that tends to send you on a guilt trip, and the outer chatter is the chatter regarding how people will judge you for the decisions you make.

Trust me, drowning out all the chatter of why you should not break free is one of the toughest things to do, but stay focused and on course. The first step is the hardest, but once you decide to, you will feel better. Each step will give you the courage to take the next. Stay strong and don't give up; you will be happy you made the effort.

There are people that will be so ready and willing to send you on a free guilt trip which you do not want to take. When someone tries to guilt trip me, my response to that is "Thank you.

This is one trip I can take on my own, and I do not wish to take it. Thank you." Surround yourself with people who uplift and encourage you on this path of self-discovery.

Setting up boundaries is important. Sometimes societal expectations can seep into our lives through the opinions and judgements of others. Don't be afraid to say no when something doesn't align with your values. You don't owe anyone an explanation for your choices. Remember: you are your own boss and you choose your own destiny. You must respect the boundaries of others as well, just as you expect others to respect yours.

To live your own life, you will need to take risks to get out of your comfort zone, break free, and try new things. You will need to be open to accepting the consequences of your actions and being okay with it and growing from the lessons.,Some people are comfortable not taking risks and prefer to stay with what they know; they like being followers, and that's totally fine for them. That is why I say it is not necessary for everyone to break free from societal norms.

Sometimes, it is worth taking risks and getting out of your comfort zone. The chances and risks you take can prove to be very rewarding. When you go on this journey of self-discovery, you will learn who your true friends are and who truly aligns with your values.

Be open and allow yourself to be flexible to what life has to offer. You may be directed to go on different courses, and your paths may change. Go with it. I know I have followed my inner guidance to lead me to where I am supposed to be. It has always led me on a course that is right for me.

Change is a wonderful experience. You never know what is ahead of you, and some of the opportunities could be just what you really want but don't know how to achieve. Don't beat yourself up if the outcome is not what you hoped for; at least you will then know not to repeat the same pattern.

You learn from making mistakes; that is what gives you the experience of how to move forward in future. You learn through experience what you like and what you don't like. Be kind to yourself when you make mistakes, because without those mistakes you won't have the experience you need to avoid making mistakes in future.

Just as you would respect others' boundaries because you expect them to respect yours, you, too, must respect others' choices, just as you would want others to respect the choices you make in life. It is okay to agree to disagree. No two people can be the same. Celebrate your uniqueness and celebrate others for their uniqueness as well.

As we go through life, we will continue to break free from social expectations because it is a continuous journey. As you grow, you change. Your values may change as you evolve. Your desires change. Life is about adapting to constant change. We learn as we grow. Be brave in shaping your own life in such a way that it will bring you joy and happiness—a life with a purpose.

## 3. Express Your Feelings

This is a topic that many of us struggle with. Many would use the excuse that they do not express their feelings for fear of hurting others' feelings, but in reality there is much more to the underlying reason for not doing so. It's a journey of self-discovery and vulnerability, but trust me when I say it's worth it. I say this because I practise speaking my truth. I have always believed in the statement "It's better to have the painful truth than a kind lie."

People that know me know that my truthful statements come from a place of love and genuine care, and they have come to appreciate that and know that when they want an honest opinion or advice, they can come to me and expect truthful answers.

Being able to speak your truth also shows others that you have integrity, which is an excellent trait to have.

There are multiple reasons why people have difficulties truly expressing themselves. Society does play a role in it, because there is an invisible expectation people tend to feel about how we must put on a brave face. Being emotional is considered to be weak. In order to avoid showing weakness, people avoid expressing what they truly feel.

In my opinion, expressing our thoughts and feelings takes courage, because we are allowing ourselves to be vulnerable and speak our truth. Having emotions is part of being human. If we do not express our thoughts and feelings when we should, we tend to bottle things inside, which ultimately has an unhealthy effect on our bodies, causing discomfort and illness.

I prefer to express myself clearly and prefer not have others trying to guess what is in my mind or how I am feeling. When I feel upset or angry, I vent it out instead of letting it brew inside. I consider holding anger within to be like letting poison linger in my system, which is not healthy for me. However, it takes a lot for me to get angry because I have the ability to see things in a way that can take me out of a place of upset or anger.

I have adopted a life of self-acceptance, which puts me in a good place. With that comes accepting others and having healthy boundaries, which prevents me from allowing others to interfere with my inner peace. Having self-respect is also a way not to allow others to infringe on your own happiness. When I express what I need when it is needed, that leaves no room for anger or resentment.

The first step to finding the strength to express your feelings is acknowledging them. We are human. It's okay to feel sad, happy, angry, or scared. Emotions are unpredictable at times, just like the weather. When you are tired and stressed, you will notice that you will be more emotional than you would be when you are well rested, and in a good frame of mind. That is why self-care is important.

If, however, you take good care of yourself, be kind to yourself, and don't beat yourself up when you are feeling emotional, take note how you react to circumstances around you when you are emotional. If your actions have caused you to have conflicts with others, go within and analyse whether your reaction was from a place of emotion and whether you may have said something hurtful to others that you did not mean. Let this be your guide for yourself.

It is best not express yourself when you are feeling emotional; you may want to practise not reacting and expressing yourself when you are no longer in an emotional state.

I prefer not to express myself when I am feeling emotional or when others are too emotional, especially when they are feeling angry. When people are in an emotional state, what is expressed is not received as it should be. I may choose not to express myself in circumstances when I feel it would serve no purpose. Maintaining silence in some matters is better for all involved.

When emotions are high, there is a potential to say something that could be hurtful, and you want to avoid that because you know for yourself that you do not really mean to be hurtful. Being human, we tend to react to protect ourselves; when we feel we are attacked, we attack back. However, when you are confident in knowing who you are, chances are that you will not fall prey to any attack dished out to you. You will not react, but rather you will have the ability to respond gracefully, maintaining your calm.

## 4. Self-Compassion and Self-Acceptance

I will be talking about self-love and self-acceptance throughout this book, and you will notice how I stress the importance of self-compassion and self-acceptance.

That is really the main purpose of why I am writing this book. It is mainly about self-awareness. I would like to help you to be more self-aware so you can identify what you need to be happy in life. What steps do you need to take in your personal goals to achieve what you want to achieve in life so you can find happiness within and feel content?

Life, as you are well aware, is not easy. It has plenty of surprises and challenges. That in itself is difficult to get through at times. When you do not accept yourself or love yourself, you are adding additional stress to your already stressful life. There is not a single person in the world who can say he or she does not encounter stress or challenges. Everyone does. You learn how to manage them so they do not have a negative impact on you—more specifically, on your health.

I would like us to dive into the topic of embracing ourselves for who we truly are and being kind to ourselves through self-compassion and self-acceptance. Life is tough enough; therefore, you do not need to make it harder for yourself by criticizing or judging your own thoughts, feelings, and actions.

We can sometimes hurt ourselves unknowingly by allowing what people say or do to hurt us even though harm is not intended on their part. When we are not aware of ourselves and our worth, we may have low self-esteem and lack confidence. When we are in such a space, what we hear and what we perceive may not be accurate, and we can misunderstand the intentions of others and may think they are saying something or doing something to hurt us.

In my practice, clients doing the healing journey with me have new awareness of how true the above statement is. As they learn to grow and have better awareness of themselves, their self-esteem and self-confidence rise, and their perception changes. They are able to discern for themselves how the ways in which they react or respond differ.

The ways they see or hear things are different because they are no longer in the victimhood mentality. They also learn to take responsibility for their own feelings and stop the blame game. They no longer blame others for how they feel, because they have a realization that a lot of their emotions and hurt are self-inflicted. Previously, they were likely unaware that they truly had control over how they think or react to situations.

We must be our own best friends by showing ourselves the same understanding and support we offer to our loved ones. It is about showing ourselves the same kindness we would show to others. Stop being hard on yourself. If you made a mistake, that is okay; just tell yourself it is okay. You will learn from the experience and will not make the same mistake again. I am sure you have said the same thing to your friends when they have been hard on themselves.

Accepting ourselves with all our flaws does not mean we do not need to make any improvements on ourselves or grow. It means we accept that we have certain flaws and we recognize it and accept that we have areas in which we can learn and grow. Personal development is important.

When you find yourself criticizing yourself or being critical and doubting yourself, be mindful of what you are doing to yourself at that moment and stop, take a deep breath, and forgive yourself for being hard on yourself. Do not get carried away in self-criticism. Remind yourself that you need to be your own best friend. You would do the same when choosing the types of friends you wish to surround yourself with. You are better off surrounding yourself with people who are supportive and kind to you in your journey of self-discovery. If there is anyone in your life who has a habit of bringing you down constantly or making you feel you are not good enough, you are best to cut ties with that person and disassociate yourself from him or her. If it is a family member it is not easy to break ties with, you may want to limit your time with that person. And when you do have to interact with him or her, it's advisable for you to set your boundaries.

You are not being selfish if you are taking care of yourself. Your mental well-being should be your priority. Do whatever is necessary for you to achieve it, but bear in mind that when I suggest that you do whatever is necessary, I mean you should do it without being hurtful to others. Spend some quality time doing things you love doing. If you have any hobby you love, spend time doing that, whether it's going out in nature for a hike, painting, hanging out with friends, sharing a meal, or doing activities together—anything that will bring you joy.

Be realistic with the goals you set for yourself so you won't beat yourself up for not achieving them. If you need to break them down into smaller steps that are manageable, so be it. But remember to celebrate your achievements, whether you want to celebrate with a friend or just on your own by treating yourself to something you always wanted. Acknowledge your achievements. Doing so will motivate you to set more goals.

Being authentic, or being true to yourself, is about being honest with yourself and about yourself. Being transparent and honest allows you to connect with others on a deeper level because when you do so you don't need to wear a mask to impress others or to fit in. You will attract people who will appreciate you for you, your genuine self.

Being open and honest shows that you possess integrity, which is a foundation of trust in any relationship. People will trust and respect you for your honesty. It can encourage others to do the same. It is not just about being honest in sharing your story but is also about accepting others for who they are and having compassion and listening to them with empathy. This shows you have a genuine interest in them.

Be willing to forgive yourself when you make mistakes, and be forgiving towards others as well. Show them understanding and that you want them to show you the same, because no one is perfect, or everyone is perfect with their imperfections. Accepting yourself with your imperfections is being kind to yourself. That is what we call self-compassion and self-acceptance.

# 5. Building Genuine Connections

What I like to talk about here is us being totally honest with ourselves. Being honest and being real means being authentic regarding who we truly are, even when our parents or family and friends expect us to be who they have in their minds. Oftentimes parents expect their children to achieve what they could not achieve themselves because of their own obstacles.

We need to be okay with who we are and be okay to live life however we wish to, even if it means we may need to disappoint our family or friends, because in the long run, if we live based on the expectations of others, we will soon feel something is missing in our lives.

When all our hopes and dreams are being squashed in order to make others happy, we soon lose the joys of life, and life may seem meaningless. Depression can set in, or even resentments towards the person or people we feel have placed their expectations on us. In such cases, people start to blame others for the expectations placed upon them.

In all honesty, no matter what expectations others may have for us, they cannot be blamed for the choices we make in how we live our lives. If you choose to meet those expectations and you are not happy, you are responsible for your own happiness.

When you choose to be authentic, you are not only being kind to yourself by being who you are and allowing yourself to be honest with others about your choices to live life as you choose; you are also being honest with them that although they may have certain expectations, you cannot meet those expectations. You thus avoid being resentful towards them for having those expectations, and you will not be holding in all your negative emotions, hurting yourself and possibly your relationships as well.

Being honest helps you to build genuine relationships and connections with others. You are willing to be transparent with your strengths and weaknesses, and in turn you will earn the respect of others for your honesty and they will value you for who you are.

Those who are in your circle will also feel the comfort and safety of being open and honest around you because they will know that you understand their need to be honest, and they know that you will not judge them and that you will accept them for who they are as well. You will learn to have better communication with each other because you will not be worried about how you need to put on a mask. You will be able to allow your communication to flow genuinely.

## 6. Masks and Pretences

When you choose to be your authentic self, you take down the mask, and you will no longer feel the need to pretend. This very choice makes you feel as if you have unloaded a heavy burden you have been carrying that was weighing you down. I always found that trying to keep up a front was more bothersome than being authentic, to be honest. I believe it is best to be yourself. If someone doesn't like me for me, it's not my loss. If people do not want to invest the time to get to know who I am, they miss out on what I have to offer. I prefer to associate with people who will accept me as I am.

Oftentimes people choose to wear masks or keep up with pretences because they want to fit in or feel accepted. Sometimes this is due to their fear of being viewed as weak if they show emotions. Keeping up with pretences, in my opinion, is hard work. In the long run, it is not possible to have meaningful relationships, because such relationships are based on lies.

I observed a group of external family members that lived with an outward appearance of being a very loving and supportive family group. Even though the entire family lived with the intentions of having a close, supportive family, they ended up being a supportive family group. What was missing was a genuine one-on-one intimate relationship. In this particular case, I can see the benefit of family support even though it may seem superficial.

I value honesty. I feel it is better to be upfront and honest no matter what the situation is. When someone triggers me, I prefer to express how I feel than to hold it in and let it fester. I feel that if I held it in, it would be like having a poison contaminate me. If someone asks for my opinion, I will give an honest answer even though I know it is not what the person wants to hear. It is better to speak the painful truth than a kind lie.

I am honest. However, in sensitive situations, I know how to be diplomatic or be gentle in the delivery of the message. I try to deliver it according to how a person receives it. Some may prefer kid gloves, while some just like direct honesty.

I do have to admit I learned this skill over the years. I used to be blunter and more direct, but I soon realized that not everyone can handle that.

I have also learned that there are some instances in which speaking my mind may be a waste of energy and will not change the circumstance, or in which the person I speak to will not appreciate what is conveyed or be willing to grow. I will not waste my breath in such cases.

I value my breath and energy and prefer to speak my mind when I know what I have to say will have a positive impact; otherwise, it would be a waste of time, energy, and breath. I consider whether speaking up will matter or be worth it. If the audience is not interested in growing or are self-centred, I distance myself politely.

You might've heard the statement "Don't waste your breath." I agree with this when it comes to people not being open to change. Their negativity can drain us. So I save my words for those who value them.

When you stop wearing a mask, you are being authentic; you are being true to yourself. You are accepting yourself as you are with all your strengths and weaknesses. You are unique just as you are with your imperfections; be proud, and be open to growth. If you need to change your weakness into strength, go ahead and make the change and grow. Remember that you are amazing, and be proud of who you are.

Keeping up with pretences or wearing masks creates a wall between you and others. When you do so, you prevent your true self from shining because the mask is blocking your inner beauty and allowing light to shine. You start attracting authentic people when you are being authentic. Like the saying "Like attracts like," you will attract people who will appreciate you and love you for who you genuinely are. These bonds are strong and valuable.

You will feel more liberated, light, and carefree because you will not have to be on guard to make sure you say just the right thing that you think others want to hear or because you are concerned about whether you can make them happy. When you are ill and tired, keeping up pretences is too much of an effort. Being authentic and honest is like finally coming out of the darkness into the light. When you do so, people get to see who you really are.

Accepting others and allowing them to see you as you really are builds self-confidence because you are telling yourself and others that" I am good as I am and I am enough."

You feel a new-found sense of inner strength, and you no longer are seeking validation from others and are trusting yourself and the decisions you make for yourself.

You begin to create a space for yourself and others that is safe. It is as though you are opening your doors and allowing others into your heart and inviting them in just as they are because you learn to respect and accept others just as they are. You learn to have healthy boundaries, and those who do not resonate with you are not part of your inner circle, thus having like-minded people who are authentic in your circle, and you deepen the connection with those around you.

It can be emotionally draining and exhausting when you feel

you have to keep up pretences and try to be someone who others expect of you instead of being the person you are. I consider pretending to be someone we are not as hard work and painful. I resigned from a job when I was told that my honesty, although appreciated, may offend new staff and that I should keep my honesty to myself.

When I was asked to reconsider my resignation, I said I would consider it with the condition that I was not asked to be someone I am not. I feel more at ease when I can operate as the person I am. Being accepted as I am is an honour and respect I value deeply.

Operating as your true self helps you to make decisions that align with your values. When you do so, you will go through life with a clearer sense of purpose and direction. It also improves your emotional and mental well-being. You offer yourself the gift of self-love and self-acceptance. You become kinder to yourself, and that ripples through all aspects of your life and to those around you. You inspire others with your examples of how you conduct yourself by being authentic and having love and compassion for yourself and others.

# Chapter 3

*Honesty and Vulnerability*

## 1. Power of Honesty

Do you remember a time when you were totally honest with someone—even yourself? Yes, I did write "yourself," because I know there are times when we can be dishonest with ourselves because we may not want to acknowledge something or not see that we have made an error. This is part of being human.

I know there have been times I probably have been guilty of not being honest with myself, because I have tried to make excuses for others and have not been honest with myself by making excuses for them. I have also refused to acknowledge the times when people took me for granted or took advantage of my kindness. I was not willing to see anything negative about people and told myself that they did not mean to be so.

Experiences have taught me that such repetitive behaviour forced me to acknowledge the facts and the truth that not everyone always has good intentions and I must stop lying to myself, stop making excuses, learn to recognize such behaviours that are not healthy for my well-being, and set up boundaries.

I, too, have oftentimes convinced myself and lied to myself

and said I am fine when I was not fine. However, I am past that now, I will acknowledge myself when I am not fine, feel it, and then move on, which is healthier and better than denying the truth. Being honest helps us genuinely feel or think without pretences, leaving no room for illusions. It truly transforms our lives in ways beyond our imagination.

I believe highly in having integrity. In order for us to have integrity, we must be honest and value our words. People know they can count on me any time because I value my words. People can rely on me and what I say.

I have been told many times that I walk the talk. I have even been told that I walked before I talked and that I do what I say I will do. When you are honest, people also trust you. Trust is an important ingredient in all relationships.

I am certain you probably will agree with me that honesty is powerful. If you are wondering why this is it so, just think about how often we suppress our opinions to avoid conflict or pretend to be someone we are not to gain approval. Even though this act may seem to be harmless, it is not all that harmless, because it becomes a burden. The more you suppress the truth, the more you get entangled in the web of lies, and then it becomes hard to break free from this vicious cycle.

Allowing others to see you as you are is so liberating because you do not need to pretend and you do not need to build walls to protect yourself.

Sharing your thoughts and feelings with others leads to deeper connections because your behaviour encourages others to break down their walls as well.

Honesty is appreciated by others, and when you are honest, they feel they can trust you, which makes you relatable and trustworthy. People appreciate me for my honesty, especially when they are seeking advice from me. They know that I will be honest and tell them what they need to hear and not what they want to hear. They also know I care enough about them to be honest with my thoughts and opinions, and that I will tell them what is best for them.

When I am at a business setting at work, I prefer to be honest with my opinions when we are in business meetings, even if it means my thoughts are totally different from those of the rest of my colleagues. I consider the best interest of the company and am not afraid to say so if I feel some solutions are better than others. But, of course, I will have supporting facts. If you do the same, you will be surprised how your courage to express your thoughts is appreciated.

Honesty is beneficial all around. When you are honest, you relieve yourself of the guilt of lying, of carrying a heavy burden, or of the pit you feel in your stomach when you are not truthful. Here I am referring to that nagging feeling of wondering what you will do when the truth comes out. Of course, some have no conscience and are chronic liars. They may not feel the weight of being dishonest, which does not apply here.

Those who have consciences feel the burdens of guilt and anxiety. When you adopt an honest lifestyle, you are free from the chains of anxiety and guilt, because there will be no need to cover up one lie with another. If you make a mistake, be honest, honestly admit it, and make the changes you need so you won't have a ball and chain weighing you down.

Some people will say it is not always easy to be honest or be transparent. Sometimes it means some conversations can be difficult or uncomfortable, such as admitting making a mistake or telling your best friend his or her behaviour or actions are hurtful without feeling that being honest could ruin your relationship with your friend or that your job could be jeopardized.

Being honest helps you to clear the air. Maybe a friend who hurt you did not intend to hurt you and will be saddened to know his or her actions hurt you unintentionally. When you are honest with such a friend, that friend will appreciate your honesty and will make an attempt to not do it again. In a work situation, you could be viewed as strong enough to own up to your mistakes, and this creates an opportunity to resolve mistakes that were made before the mistakes create a bigger issue. In the long run, honesty can save lots of grief, heartaches, and headaches.

You need to be honest with yourself as much as you are honest with others. Sometimes you may lie to yourself by believing that you are fine when you really are not. Pretending that your problems do not exist does not make them disappear or not exist. Many people have a habit of sweeping things under the rug, thinking that if they do not see the problem, it won't be there. But the reality is that no matter how much you want to avoid it, the more it will haunt you. So you might as well face it head-on.

Being honest with yourself helps you to face your issues and confront them. Being honest does not always mean acknowledging your insecurities, fears, or mistakes. Just remember that you are human and as humans, we all make mistakes at some point in our lives. We all experience fears and challenges. These help to give you the opportunities to grow and learn when you face them.

Be honest with what you really want in life. Do you honour yourself and follow your own life path, or are you following the wishes of your parents or family members? In the earlier years of my life, my parents had full control of my life because that is how we were raised. I went to college to major in commerce and economics because my mum expected me to be an accountant.

Being in college at the age of fifteen and living a sheltered life, I did not know any better. I did not know much about being true to myself, because it was a normal expectation that we live the life that was mapped out for us.

Admitting that I did not know much about being true to myself felt scary and embarrassing, but it allowed me to become aware and to learn that I did have a choice to live the life I wanted. This helped me to make choices that were aligned with my genuine desires of my own path, and I adopted a career totally different from what was intended for me by my family members.

I followed my heart and now am doing what I truly want in my life, and that is being in service to others, helping others, and making a positive impact on the lives I touch.

I feel that following my heart, speaking my truth, and living the life following the path I feel I am meant to be on makes my life very worthwhile, and I feel happy with the choices I make, and helping others to find their inner light, which guides them to their happiness, is so rewarding.

## 2. Vulnerability as a Strength

People are under the impression that the ability to maintain emotions is a strength. But true strength lies in not letting emotions dictate our actions. The ability to show emotions or vulnerability is not a weakness, but the ability to show emotions and be vulnerable is a strength because it takes great strength to be able to be transparent to others and be authentic.

Being open about your fears and insecurities can make you stronger because you are allowing yourself to overcome the fears of being judged, not liked, or rejected. When you let your guard down or take down your protective wall, you show your real self and indirectly give others permission to do the same, which helps to build mutual trust.

When you allow yourself to open up and share that you are struggling with some issues, you can create a bond with others who can resonate with what you are going through, because they can relate with it and identify with themselves that they, too, are going through something similar. You can then begin to share your experiences and provide support for each other and end up building a bond with each other. Such experiences make relationships deeper and more meaningful.

This is what I encourage in the workshop I facilitate, where all those present feel comfortable sharing and know they are in a safe space to do that. They realize they are not alone in life's struggles and can support each other by bringing in shared comfort to be open and honest and learn to be confident in accepting who they are.

When you tell yourself that you won't let your fears hold you back any more, you allow yourself to step out of your comfort zone and talk about things that you were once afraid to talk about. You allow yourself to grow, learn, change, and discover a new side of you that you didn't know existed inside of you.

Allowing yourself to be able to be vulnerable in your professional life is also valuable. It is not only all about being vulnerable in your personal life. A good leader or manager is someone who is willing to be vulnerable and is willing to admit that he or she does not know it all and is happy to accept suggestions and willing to work as a team and work together.

A good leader is open to growth. In order to grow, one must be willing to be open to vulnerability. A strong leader embraces his or her own vulnerability and is open to his or her own imperfections, which allows the team permission to be who they are and accept themselves to be who they are. Such an environment gives everyone the feeling of comfort and safety to share their thoughts and ideas, allowing wonderful things to happen.

In such a setting, you won't feel the anxiety of not being perfect or afraid to make mistakes, because in a culture where you are allowed to be who you are, you won't feel the burden of making mistakes but will rather feel that together you can help each other to find solutions to correct any mistakes or issues that may arise.

Being transparent or exposing your vulnerabilities may be scary because it can cause you to fear that you will be judged or that people will think less of you if they know everything about you. This is because you feel insecure about yourself. You may be quite surprised to know that what you fear is not what reality is. Instead you may find that people are actually supportive and let you know you are not alone in what you feel or experience, so instead of pushing you away, they may draw you closer and be supportive in your journey.

Allowing yourself to be honest and vulnerable is a lifelong journey. You will continue throughout your life with various experiences and situations in which life will continue to test you to be your authentic self. You will take each step as it comes and be okay with being uncomfortable with what you are going through and the emotions you will deal with, and you will go through your life's journey dealing with circumstances as they come up. This will help you to be empowered and stronger.

## 3. Difficult Conversations with Grace

Having conversations on delicate topics or of a sensitive nature is often difficult, and I have known people to avoid such conversations to avoid being misunderstood or to prevent conflicts. But what people do not realize is that silence can lead to misunderstanding because it can be mistaken as a lack of empathy or concern.

Sometimes difficulties arise due to differences in beliefs or perspectives and emotions that contribute to our interactions.

We have a tendency to shy away from conversations when we feel we need to be open and tell the truth in sharing our thoughts to avoid hurting others, as we may not agree with the opinions of others, and these type of conversations could bring up strong emotions. It is these strong emotions that make it hard for people to bring up such conversations.

The anticipation of what emotions it may trigger is the reason why people avoid having such heavy conversations and how it will affect their relationships going forward.

Being graceful in communicating is not about ignoring issues or avoiding arguments. It is about understanding and valuing the feelings of others and respecting their viewpoints that could be different to your own. It is about being open to hearing different perspectives and respecting them.

We must be willing to agree to disagree. Choosing words carefully helps us to avoid any misunderstanding by being kind and compassionate in how we speak to others. Allow each other to speak without fear of getting into heated arguments, allowing each to feel safe to have open communication, and respect each other's viewpoints.

I tend to play out scenarios in my head and prepare myself mentally prior to any conversation that is difficult to have, especially since we never know how a person will react to what we have to say. Being calm while having conversations helps me in delivering the message I will deliver.

Calmness will generally put the listener at ease and cause him or her to be less defensive, which helps the communication to be easy and smooth. Mind you, there are always exceptions to the rule. In order for us to have effective communication, we must be willing to listen actively. Sometimes people focus on what they want to say and do not absorb what is being said.

Active listening means paying full attention to the speaker and what he or she is saying so we can truly hear and understand his or her point of view. It shows respect and encourages empathetic and productive communication.

When we adopt empathy while we communicate, we are able to connect with others on a deeper level. This means we are allowing ourselves to feel what they may feel and to try to understand their views and perspective. As an empath, this comes to me naturally. I feel what others feel without even trying. But those who are not born empaths can develop empathy by trying to understand others' perspectives and imagining themselves in similar situations to comprehend what others may be feeling or how they might react. Sometimes knowing the nature of the other person helps you to understand what he or she may feel.

When discussing a sensitive topic, it's best to express yourself by explaining how you would feel in similar situations. This approach prevents others from feeling defensive. They will be more willing to listen because they won't feel the need to be on guard and will be open to what is being said.

Being calm is often the key to a difficult conversation. Speaking in a calm tone and showing respect to the person you are having a conversation with, even when you disagree with him or her, will lead to a mutually respectful conversation.

I am generally calm in most situations and am often told that my presence calms people down. My friends, colleagues, and past employers often tell me that they feel calm around me. Especially when they are dealing with lots of stress in their lives, they feel calm when they see me.

Remaining calm helps us navigate through difficult situations as well. When we are faced with problems, it is easier to solve problems by focusing on the resolution than by pointing fingers at others. People come together and collaboratively work on solutions they both will be happy with.

There will be times when we are going through rough patches in our lives. When you are feeling very emotional, it is best to step back, take a break, and allow yourself to let the emotion settle so your mind is in a clearer state to approach difficult situations, which is better for all involved. I don't believe in entering any heavy conversations when I am feeling emotional and know that I may not be in the right frame of mind to do so. I prefer to wait till I am calm so it's easier to analyse the situation and address it in a calmer and better frame of mind.

Making assumptions often leads to misunderstanding. It is best not to make assumptions about what a person may be thinking; it is better to openly ask and clarify what a person is trying to say, which will prevent any misunderstandings that may lead to conflict.

When I communicated with my son when he was a child, as young as two to three years old, I communicated with him just as I would with anyone, knowing he could understand. However, I would ask him to relay back to me what he understood, to confirm my message was understood correctly.

During any conversation of a delicate nature, it is always best to clarify what is being conveyed to avoid any misunderstandings. Having a clear understanding of what is being said leaves both parties with a positive outcome that can help with any future conversations. It is also important to have the attitude of gratitude when you experience a positive impact from your difficult conversations. Show your appreciation for your relationships and demonstrate willingness and openness to work through difficult challenges together.

The ability to have a positive outcome from a difficult conversation of a sensitive nature is not an innate talent for all. This is a skill one chooses to learn to master when one cares about oneself and the relationships one has with people in one's life. It is up to us to choose how we want to interact with others. When we care enough for the people in our lives, we are willing to learn and grow, and we make the effort to communicate with others with grace and compassion.

We will continually encounter difficult and sensitive situations throughout our journeys in life, and we cannot avoid going through different phases. We will continue to have those moments when we have conversations that are difficult, but as we grow through these life moments, we will learn through experiences to have the skills to have graceful communication. We learn to have the skill to do so because of our willingness to grow and transform through the challenges we go through in our lives, and we learn to surround ourselves with people who are also open to learning and growing.

## 4. Healing and Growth

Our lives are filled with stories of happy days and painful moments. I do not believe that anyone's life is so perfect that he or she does not have any challenges. Even those who have things going easy for them in life will experience some challenges. Meanwhile, those who have many life struggles may consider those very challenges as nothing. Everyone perceives challenges differently. What is a challenge for one may not be for someone else.

Being open—sharing your thoughts and feelings—can help you heal and grow. There was a time in my life when I was married and I was ashamed to talk about what I was going through. I did not know how common it was for others to be living lives filled with challenges or abuse. I lived a very sheltered life before that. Our family, both immediate and extended, never spoke about any private or personal experiences. It is not common to share personal stories in my culture.

Opening up your thoughts and feelings can free you. When you share your feelings with people you trust, you don't have to carry them all alone. It's not weak to do this. In time, in order to heal, I learned that I needed to talk about my experiences to help me analyse what I was going through. I found that these experiences were, in fact, not acceptable, and that I could do something to help myself. It takes courage to open up and talk about painful experiences through tears. People often assume that tears show weakness, but they actually show how strong you are.

Healing takes place when we can talk about our painful experiences. It helps us to hear our own stories, which gives us the aha moments that can motivate us to help heal from our traumatic situations. When you open up, you let people understand you better. This helps you feel connected instead of being alone. Sharing your feelings is the start of healing.

When I first learned to open up and start to talk about my pain and experiences, I was able to put some pieces of the puzzle together as to why I felt the way I did. I gained a better picture of what was going on in my life that was affecting me in ways that it did. When the pictures started to become clearer, I had a better understanding of what to do to heal from my circumstances.

Sometimes sharing your experience hurts. Since I did not have anyone I felt I could truly trust to talk to at the time about something so personal, it was not easy for me. Because of my difficult pregnancy, I was under the care of a public health nurse, who became aware of what I was going through in my life at that time and encouraged me to share my experiences. I had an aha moment when I shared.

Also, talking about your pain makes you feel stronger. It's like looking at your fears and saying, "I'm not scared of you any more." It's tough, but it helps you feel better in the end. Your pain becomes like a story of how you got better.

When you're okay with not being perfect, you can grow a lot. Admitting that you need to get better isn't bad. It actually helps you get better. You grow from facing your challenges head-on. Think of it as a plant. A plant grows when it reaches for the sun and the sky. Similarly, you grow when you try new things and learn from them. When you say, "I want to learn and change," you start growing. You might meet new people, face challenges, or learn about yourself.

You start to have a better understanding of yourself as you learn to share more about yourself. In the process, you are slowly and gradually bringing down the walls you have built for yourself. You start to show who you really are because you no longer have a mask on. Being open, you are removing all the things that prevented you from being exposed.

As I opened myself up to becoming who I am and who I really wanted to be, I felt as if I had broken down the walls, come out of my shell, and allowed my true self to shine. I am now proud to let my light shine bright. It feels so liberating to be my own person. I no longer feel restricted by cultural and societal expectations.

Because of my openness and my comfort of being who I am and speaking my truth, people have the impression of me as a fearless person, which is far from the truth. I do have fears like everyone else; I simply do not allow them to restrict me from moving forward as I should.

Healing from life's trauma is a journey. Healing and growing is not an instant trip or a quick short trip, but it is a journey that takes lots of hard work and determination, because learning to accept yourself for who you are and being comfortable being you takes you through various steps of overcoming the obstacles that prevent you from accepting yourself.

I learned to accept myself with all my imperfections and turned those imperfections into something positive, which helped me grow and become stronger. Now I am helping others do the same in their healing journeys.

## 5. Authentic Communication in Relationships

I believe strongly about being authentic in our relationships and communications. I am repeatedly mentioning this throughout this book because I want to be sure you understand the importance of being your real you. By being true and transparent and authentic, we allow our true selves to shine. Being authentic is more important than you might think.

When you are being authentic, you no longer need to try to impress others so they may like you, because you are basically announcing the fact that you are happy being who you are: "Take me as I am. This is me with all my gifts and imperfections that make me unique."

There is no longer a need to pretend to be someone you are not. I never liked pretending to be someone I am not. In fact, I refuse to be someone I am not. If anyone cannot accept me for who I am, it is his or her loss. I have no desire to change to fit anyone's expectations, because I am well aware of what I have to offer the world, and there is a lot that I do offer.

Being authentic in any relationship is so important. It promotes trust. And when we are honest and being authentic, we start to attract those who will appreciate us for who we truly are. Without trust, relationships are meaningless. Having trust in a relationship provides you with the feeling of being safe and understood, and allows you to be valued for who you are. You never have to worry whether you are saying the right thing or not, because those who understand and care about you will understand what you want to convey to them.

When you speak from the heart, you have a deeper connection. Your words carry sincerity and emotion, making your message powerful.

Think about your best friend. What makes that bond strong? It's probably the fact that you can be yourself around him or her. In an authentic relationship, you feel safe, understood, and valued. When you have a heart-to-heart conversation, you allow yourself to open up and share your dreams and aspirations. These types of conversations stay with you for a long time. There will be times when you will reminisce about those moments you shared in your friendships which are so special, and sharing those moments once again will cement your bond even more.

I recall the day a friend and I skipped school in the afternoon after lunch. She needed a friend to talk to about what she was going through. Neither of us was the type to miss classes, nor were we ones disobey rules, but we did that day, as my friend needed a friend to share her feelings with.

That is the day our friendship grew, and we bonded and became friends for life. She was there for me when I needed someone to talk to. We share a special bond because we feel safe and comfortable with each other to be vulnerable and be our true selves. Today, thirty-eight years later, in 2023, we are still friends, and we are able to be honest with each other. Sometimes we are fine hearing a painful truth. We accept it because we know it comes from a place of love and respect.

When you are authentic, you are basically breaking the walls that separate you from others. Being vulnerable is showing the side of you that most people are not comfortable showing, the softer side, because most of the time people like to show they are strong and confident. I recall a friend saying to me, "I feel I need to be honest with you because you are always honest with me." People feel comfortable being authentic and honest because they know that they won't be judged and know that everyone has his or her own weaknesses and struggles he or she goes through, and that that is perfectly fine.

Openness amongst people allows everyone the feeling of comfort and the ability to learn and grow from each other. By sharing stories and feedback with everyone being authentic about their viewpoints, people opening doors of communication and understanding of different perspectives, growth, and acceptance, even when they do not see eye to eye, because they know they can learn from each other. It is about respecting differences while being true to yourself.

Family expectations and society often influence people to conform and try to fit in. Most often people conform to these expectations because it feels it is easier to do so to avoid conflict and the feeling of the need to fit in or be liked. However, if you feel you find these expectations to be restrictive, you will feel uncomfortable because your core self wants to be who you are, wants to accept yourself, and truly wants others to accept you. Being authentic isn't always easy; you have to want to accept yourself first in order for you to have the courage to break free from all these restrictive expectations.

I am sure there have been times when you didn't speak up because you were afraid of what others might think. It is very common for people to feel this; you are not the only one. Don't be afraid to speak up and have your voice be heard. Allow yourself to be heard and seen for who you are—the authentic you. Once people get to know this is how you are, you know you are not pretending and are able to see your true intentions and that you are being genuine. This builds trust. Others will come to feel they can count on you and that you will not disappoint them, which is a comfort for them to know.

Imagine a friendship in which you always know where you stand. My friend I spoke of earlier who was my classmate, in our initial friendship stage, said to me, "You are so honest, and it is painful to hear the truth. I know it hurts to hear the truth, but I appreciate it because I will always know where I stand with you." In such a friendship, there are no guessing games because you both communicate authentically. That trust allows your relationship to flourish. Because of how I conduct myself honestly, I have established strong bonds with people in my circle. They know my words have weight.

Authenticity is about being authentic throughout your life and not as a temporary phase; nor is it about being authentic with a select few. When you are honest about your strengths and weaknesses, you become more self-aware, and it helps you accept the choice to grow in areas in which you want to improve and better yourself. It becomes your tool for personal growth that leads to creating deep bonds with the people in your life. Speak from your heart, and let the truth brighten your world.

## 6. Honesty with Empathy

Do you find that being honest conflicts or clashes with your desire to be kind and considerate? If so, you will need to be creative and balance honesty with empathy. It takes a special skill to be able to have a conversation where you can be compassionate. You can learn the skill if you so wish. I know it is possible. I know that in my younger years, I was blunt. People still tell me that I shoot from the hip.

As I journey through life, I know that there are occasions when some situations are very sensitive, and it is important that we need to be gentler yet honest. I have learned to be more selective and careful with how I choose my words so I can be kind and compassionate yet be honest. We can be selective with our words when we are calm and collected.

It is a conscious decision to not allow triggers to affect our peace of mind for us to be in calm states. To be able to know what can trigger us, we must learn to be self-aware and identify what our triggers are. I think that at a very young age I found it pointless to argue with anyone when they he or she was not making sense. In situations like that, I chose not to react. Rather, I would absorb what was being said by the other party when he or she was angry.

I would just listen and not react or respond till the storm had passed, then I would address it by letting the other party know that he or she was behaving irrationally.

This helps to promote honest and straightforward communication without hiding anything, resulting in no one being on the defensive. When you're empathetic, you understand where someone is coming from and care about his or her feelings. It's like saying, "I get it, and I'm here for you." Being an empath myself, I take empathy to the next level. Empaths can connect with others even more so than most; we can feel people's physical and emotional pain.

We are like human lie detectors; we often can detect when people are not being authentic. However, this is not 100 per cent foolproof, because some people have such a thick mask on that we, too, can be fooled by them. As an empath, I do sense and feel others quite accurately and am able to navigate with people well.

During the Healing Journey Program sessions with my clients, I guide them to consider putting themselves in another person's shoes to help them to try and comprehend what the other person may be feeling or thinking, or where he or she is coming from, and not to make judgements or wrong assumptions. They learn to listen actively, understand, and respond accordingly. Through the Healing Journey Program, they learn the skills to be self-aware, to have different perspectives, and to see the bigger picture to avoid misunderstanding.

When someone comes to me and asks me how I like his or her new hairstyle, I tell the person honestly, if I do not like it, that we have different tastes, and I proceed to tell him or her my thoughts on the style itself. If it suits the person, I describe how the style enhances their features. If it does not suit the person, I describe how it does not work. But if it is a style the person loves, that is all that should matter, because the person needs to feel comfortable with his or her choice, and no one else's opinion should matter.

People I know are so accustomed to my honesty that they know that I am expressing my thoughts and opinions, and that there is no ill intention behind it, and they are never offended by my honesty. It is best not to lie about your opinions; choose words to express yourself that will be respectful of others' feelings while at the same time being honest about your own taste, which may be different to theirs.

If you cultivate such a relationship with people around you with total honesty, you never have to worry that being honest will be hurtful, because it will be accepted graciously and gratefully,

It is always best to be careful how you choose your words in situations that are sensitive in nature rather than blurting out the first thing that comes to mind. I am sure we all have been guilty of that. I know that I am generally cautious, even though I am known to be brutally honest. Some say it's a gift I have of being able to be brutally honest yet have my statements received very well. I guess this may be because when people are with me, they feel "You get what you see." There is no hidden agenda. Along with the words we choose, the tones we use also help people know that our honesty comes from compassion or love.

However, everyone is different. Some prefer harsh truth as

opposed to the kid gloves. Personally, I prefer the raw, honest truth. I generally handle the truth with people in the ways they receive it. Being an empath, I have the gift of knowing how people accept what is being said. If you're delivering tough news or giving critical feedback, acknowledge the other person's feelings. Let the person know you understand that it might be hard for him or her to hear. If your honesty might be difficult to take in, make sure the other person knows you're there to support him or her. This can soften the impact of your words.

Be ready to listen empathetically when others share their thoughts or feelings. Just as you want to express yourself honestly, give the other person the chance to do the same. Balancing honesty with empathy isn't always easy, but it's worth the effort. When we communicate with honesty, we build trust in our relationships. When we do it with empathy, we show that we care about the other person's feelings. When we combine the two, we are able to have a heartfelt conversation.

# Chapter 4

*Trusting Your Heart's Compass*

## 1. Values and Beliefs

WE ALL HAVE OUR OWN PERSONAL VALUES AND BELIEFS WE LIVE by. Sometimes our values are what shape our character or traits. They help us through times of struggles and challenges to make decisions, and shape us to be the people we are. I would like for you to get to know yourself better.

To do that, we will have to dig into your beliefs and values. You will want to know what matters and why. Examples of some of these values that you may have are honesty, integrity, compassion, kindness, tolerance, and self-respect. Each person will prioritize these values differently. For example, person A may consider being honest as their first priority; meanwhile, person B may consider being compassionate to be his or her first priority.

Everyone has his or her own set of values; these are principles that give meaning to our lives. These values shape our thoughts and behaviours and how we interact with others. Beliefs, on the other hand, influence our attitudes and shape our reality. Beliefs could be cultural, religious, or political (e.g., cultural beliefs, the belief of self and identity, the belief of free will, moral belief, or belief in the afterlife). These are thoughts and convictions we have about ourselves and others. These beliefs are like the lenses through which we perceive the world.

When you understand your values and beliefs, it is like discovering your own treasure map. Your sets of values and beliefs give you a clear understanding of your purpose in life. You have a sense of direction helping you to make decisions that align with your true self. This self-awareness helps you to have a more fulfilling life because you can identify what you need to make you happy.

Think of what really matters to you in terms of values and principles, and allow yourself time to think about whom in your life you admire greatly, and why? What is it about them that you like or admire? What qualities do they possess that you respect? This is like taking a moment of self-reflection and narrowing down the list of values that you see in others that resonate the most with you. Examining what you like in others and what resonates with you helps you to define the person you wish to be and what values you wish to carry throughout your life.

I have done workshops in which we wrote a list of values and then later on narrowed it down to our core value by prioritizing the choices.

Reflect on moments when you felt the happiest and most fulfilled, as well as times when you faced challenges. What values were at play during those experiences? These moments often reveal your core values. Pay attention to how you react emotionally to various situations.

Your values often surface as strong emotions, guiding you towards what truly matters. This is why I stress teaching self-awareness—because it is the key to being aware of your emotions and your reactions to the various situations you encounter. Do you feel moved by certain songs or movies, or certain books or stories? What are the common themes and principles that resonate with you? These common themes or principles will provide you with clues to your values.

In some circumstances, you may want to ask yourself whether something is your belief or an opinion. Or is it based on facts? Try to understand and analyse where your beliefs come from. Are they from your own personal experiences or from your family or culture? Understanding where your beliefs originated will help you to differentiate between those you choose for yourself and those you inherited.

Be open to evolving your beliefs. As you gain new experiences and insights, some beliefs may shift, making way for more empowering ones. When you feel negative thoughts creep in, replace them with positive thoughts or affirmations. Giving my clients affirmations tailored to their circumstances has helped them tremendously. A simple affirmation, such as "Today I will make my day a good day," allows them to consciously choose to make the day a good day, helping to keep any negative thoughts or behaviours at bay.

Simply using this affirmation daily can reshape your perspective and your life. Many of my students have experienced the benefits of the daily affirmations that I encouraged them to create for themselves based on what their needs are. Socialize with people who support your positive belief and those who will uplift you. As you grow personally and spiritually, you start to vibrate at a higher frequency, and you will attract more people that are positive and have values similar to yours.

Consider your values when you are faced with choices. Determine whether they resonate with your values or not. Making decisions that resonate with your values will lead to greater satisfaction and confidence. Friendships built on shared values are often enduring and give you a deep sense of connection.

When your actions and values do not match, you will feel you are not being authentic, and this can cause inner turmoil. When your actions and way of living align with your values, this brings you a sense of inner peace, just as when your job aligns with your values and your work brings you a sense of purpose and satisfaction and is no longer simply a source for a paycheque.

Your values guide you through difficult times. They help you find meaning even in your darkest moments. They provide you with a strong foundation during difficult times. The journey to the path of discovering your values and beliefs is lifelong. Remember: this is a continuous process as you navigate through life's twists and turns.

Self-discovery is also a lifelong journey. Be patient with yourself through the process. Be curious and be open to learning in your approach to self-discovery. As you journey through life, you will find that some of the beliefs that you had may no longer serve you as you grow and have different perspectives in life. As you evolve, your beliefs, too, will evolve. Celebrate every step towards your new values and beliefs. Let your values be your guiding stars, and remember that everyone's journey is different and yours is unique to you. Embrace your own journey that will lead you to a life of fulfilment and joy.

## 2. Following Your Heart

Do you feel that life is a mystery and that you do not have a map to follow as you journey through life, just as children do not come with an instruction manual? Every parent learns how to raise his or her children through observing and following his or her instincts or heart. Life does not have a definite road map, as every individual has his or her own unique path to follow. Use your heart as your true north to guide you as you journey through life.

Following your heart's true north means listening to your voice and your intuition letting them guide you through life's adventures. I have always trusted and followed my intuition and inner guidance. There were times I did not follow it, only later to find out that I should have followed my instincts. I can safely assume you may have experienced this yourself when you felt you should have followed what you thought you should have done.

Following your heart or your inner guidance is like having an internal compass pointing you in the direction that often feels right. Your heart and your values help you to make choices that lead toward your dreams and passions that make you feel alive. When you feel alive because of the choices you make, this is a clue that your heart is pointing to your true north.

Your heart is not only your true north but is also that quiet, reassuring voice within you, your own true friend offering you advice in a gentle, honest way, uniquely attuned to you and your needs. It knows what is best for you, even if it goes against external pressure or opinion. It can at times be loud and clear, and at other times it can be a soft, gentle voice guiding you. Remember: listening to your heart is like having a coach by your side, helping you as your personal guide. We all have our angels and guides that regularly help us through our inner voices.

Although following your heart may feel like it leads you to what aligns with you, it does not mean that you will not encounter any challenges. It may even lead you to an area where there are uncertainties or areas where you may feel fearful, but what you need to remember is that no matter what, even if the paths may not be clear, the compass still works. Your heart will guide you to face your fears and challenges by taking risks to go forward with the guidance. You will know that your heart is leading you to a deeper purpose that aligns with you.

When I decided to practise reiki and reflexology, my purpose was to help others to heal their physical pain and discomfort. I followed my inner guidance and went with where my heart and inner guidance led me in this journey of getting into holistic healing. It led me to a different direction which I never even considered when I first got into holistic healing. I never imagined that I would be using these modalities of healing to help others heal emotionally and mentally, which ultimately improves their physical health. Doing what I do now feels like I am doing something that has a deeper and greater purpose.

Following your heart's true north means dedicating time and effort to what you love, which I feel I am doing by truly helping others as I have always wanted to do all my life.

Take the time to follow your heart. Do what you love, whether it be painting, writing, or gardening—anything that brings you joy, anything that you are passionate about. Your passion is your navigation system; that will lead you to your sense of purpose and fulfilment.

I am sure you may know that people you encounter like to compare or expect certain things. When this occurs, it is best to be true to yourself by following your heart and being authentic, even if it means that you may be different or stand out. It may not be comfortable to stand out and be different. It takes courage to be able to be true to yourself and to accept yourself as someone that does not fit in with the crowd.

I remember a time I was with my son when he was four years old. He had never liked chocolate, but one day he came home saying he loved it. I talked with him about it because I was worried he might just be saying that to fit in with his friends at school. I assured him that it was okay to be different—that even if he was the only one who didn't like chocolate at school, that would be fine. I told him that being unique is special and he doesn't have to be like everyone else. I explained that it takes strength to be yourself, even if it means standing out.

He understood and realized it's okay to be different. A few years later, he confidently told me that a friend called him weird for not liking chocolate. He didn't mind and stayed honest about his feelings. He learned to be truthful and face the outcomes, which I always appreciated and praised him for. My ability to sense honesty as an empath might have encouraged him to be honest too.

Be true to yourself, even if it means that you do not fit in with everyone else. Accepting being different is a brave and wonderful thing. It's about being authentic, being unique, and having the courage to stand out. Doubts have a way of creeping in from time to time, and you may ask yourself whether you are making the right choice when you are making a decision or whether you are capable of reaching your goals by following your inner guidance. It is very normal and natural to have doubts at times. Listen to them and then let them go. Trust yourself, and go with the flow to where your guidance is leading you, even when doubts may surface.

As you journey through life, change will be your constant companion. Let your heart be the compass to guide you in your journey. When your choices resonate with your heart, you experience inner peace and harmony. This harmony influences your interactions, your work, and your overall well-being. Your heart will guide you through life's shifts and changes. When you trust your inner guidance, accepting the changes you encounter in life becomes easier. You learn to adapt and find new directions, which helps you to be resilient.

Navigating and listening to intuition is a key component of the Healing Journey Program I offer. The first part of a six-part workshop on tapping into intuition is available on the JacintaHealingArts YouTube channel. Learning to trust and follow your heart's compass can help relieve anxiety in decision-making.

It may not always be easy or the easiest path, but it will help you through life's challenges and keep you aligned to your authentic self—a path that is filled with purpose, joy, and fulfilment. I have been told that they learned tools from me to navigate through life, similar to a compass that leads them in the right direction.

Remember to listen to that gentle voice within, accept the changes that come your way, and honour your passion. Your heart's true north will always be your constant companion. It is your most reliable source of direction in your life's journey.

## 3. Making Decisions

The Healing Journey Program helps the students to identify their core values or principles through self-discovery and peeling off layers after layers like an onion to get to the root of who they truly are. Oftentimes people lose themselves in the process of pleasing others. Discovering your core principles involves peeling back the layers of everyday life to uncover what truly matters to you.

Take time to ask yourself what you stand for. What are your beliefs, and what qualities do you hold significant in life? Your core principles will often influence your decisions. Go back and reflect on the decisions you have made in life; you will find that the decisions you made came from your underlying principles. Take notes when you are making any decisions regarding how you feel or what you feel when making them.

Decisions made from your core principles often lead to results that will feel right for you. You're then more likely to achieve goals that align with your values. When faced with a decision, outline your options. Think about how each choice aligns with you and your principles. Does one option resonate more strongly than the others? Reflect on how each option works.

Listen to your gut feelings. Your intuition often reflects the subtle nudges of your core principles, guiding you towards the right choice. Be open to seeking advice from trusted friends or family members. Sharing what you are dealing with and your dilemma with others can offer fresh perspectives that align with your principles. Focus on what truly matters.

The importance of paying attention to all the subtle changes my students experience has been consistently stressful to them, as those changes can reveal a lot about them. Do you experience a sense of alignment and peace when your choices resonate with your values? Your emotions can oftentimes guide you to your core principles.

Is there someone you admire in your life? What qualities does that person possess that resonates with you? These qualities can offer insights into your own core principles. Consider them as a lighthouse shining light upon your path ahead. When you base your decisions on these principles, you create a sense of clarity and purpose in your life.

When you make your decisions based on your own principles, you are being true to yourself. You're not trying to be someone you're not, and this authenticity radiates through your choices. It also gives you a sense of confidence. Further, it will help you to face challenges head-on. When you encounter obstacles, your principles become a source of strength. They remind you why you're making certain choices and encourage you to persevere.

Reflect on the various options when making decisions. Think of how each option makes you feel, which options resonate with you strongly, and how each choice aligns with you. Those subtle nudges are your core principles guiding you.

Sharing your dilemma with others can offer fresh perspectives that align with your principles. Focus on what truly matters.

While making decisions based on your principles can be rewarding, challenges may arise. Remember: it's okay to stand by your principles. It's your life and your journey; do what feels right for you. Others may give you good advice. You are the only person who can make the right decision for you.

## 4. Trusting Yourself

I am sure you know by now how unpredictable life can be. You feel you are not sure what to do or where to go sometimes. You have a special gift within you. Your self-confidence and your inner guidance are your gifts that will guide you when things get confusing or challenging. Use these gifts to help you make decisions when things are not clear.

Your self-confidence is your best friend because it will help you when you are not sure about something, especially when you feel unsure or feel confused. In times like this, it is best to reflect on a time when you made good choices, or decisions you made that were the right ones. Remind yourself how you felt when you were going through tough times; you didn't give up. Because you are strong, you listened to the little voice inside of you.

Your gut feelings will guide you in directions that are good for you even if things may not seem to be going perfectly. In time you will realize that it in fact was good for you, and you will be glad that you made the right choice. No one ever has all the answers, so do not worry if you feel you do not have an answer right away. Take your time to figure things out, especially when you are faced with a difficult decision.

When faced with a difficult decision, I strive to find a balance between my heart and mind to avoid regrets. I want to make sure I am not making a decision based solely on my emotions or my mind. Tell yourself, "You can do this" or "It's okay, you're trying your best."

Challenging times often tend to teach you important things. They are lessons to help you become stronger. When you are faced with uncertain times, you may feel as if you are in a fog and need a special lantern to guide your way. That is self-awareness.

Reflect on what your values are, what matters to you, and what is important—how you feel inside. Your feelings will tell you what you really want.

Sometimes you may have to dive deep within you because that is where you know things; that's where your inner voice resides. Personally, I like to go for a walk in nature or go for a drive. I do my best thinking when driving aimlessly along country roads, as there are no other distractions, and absorbing the view of nature helps me think.

Be open to learning. I love constantly learning. Like a sponge, I want to absorb as much information as possible—even on topics I may not initially be interested in. I often find myself developing interests in things I once thought I had no interest in. Think of every situation as an opportunity to learn. You can grow smarter with every experience.

Doing something different can be fun and exciting. Learn to be open and be adventurous; that's how you learn more. Instead of worrying, focus on finding solutions. It makes you feel stronger. I like to find solutions to problems instead of worrying about them. Celebrate every success and be proud of it; even tiny successes are worth celebrating. They show you're making progress.

## 5. Boundaries

One of the important topics taught in the Healing Journey Program is honouring your boundaries and trusting your intuition. It's like offering you a protective shield for you to protect yourself and a compass to guide you.

It is important to be your own best friend and to protect yourself to guide you to your happy place. Imagine having a protective shield and an inner compass that help you navigate life's challenges. Together they guide you to make choices that feel right and keep you safe.

In this journey, you are guided to understand the importance of recognizing your limits and valuing your instincts, as well as how embracing these tools empowers you to live a more authentic and fulfilling life. Think of your boundaries as an invisible fence around you. They define what is okay and what's not okay for you. Understanding and respecting these boundaries is like creating a safe space where you feel comfortable and respected.

Think about those times and situations where you felt comfortable and those where you didn't. These feelings can help you understand your boundaries. Pay attention to how you feel around others or in various situations. If something feels off, it might be a sign of a boundary being crossed. I can never stress enough how we must pay attention to every minute detail that happens in our lives so we can be more aware.

It's okay to say no when you're not comfortable with something. Being honest about your feelings helps you set and maintain your boundaries. Your boundaries protect your emotional and physical well-being. They help you avoid things that could hurt you. Quite often people get so lost in pleasing others that they forget about themselves and get taken for granted and are taken advantage of, and it in turn they hurt themselves. By not honouring their boundaries and trying to please everyone else, they lose not only their confidence and self-respect; they lose themselves.

Honouring your boundaries and trusting your intuition prevents you from losing yourself. You may think that if you please others, they will like you more, but this is not true. People like and respect those who know who they are and those who respect their own boundaries, even though initially it may not seem so. Trust me, when you set up your boundaries and honour them, you will earn more respect. I know this because I am speaking from experience personally and have also witnessed this and heard from my students how their relationships have changed and improved when they set up healthy boundaries for themselves, as well as how life became easier when they followed their intuition.

Sometimes the universe sends you little signs or feelings. These can guide you in making decisions that feel right. Intuition doesn't always give instant answers. Be patient and give yourself time to understand what your inner voice is saying. I follow my intuitive guide daily.

Respecting your boundaries and trusting your intuition have incredible benefits that empower you. When you honour your boundaries and listen to your intuition, you're being true to yourself. Setting and maintaining boundaries helps you build healthy relationships. People will respect you for valuing your well-being.

When you trust your intuition, it boosts your confidence. You become more certain about your decisions; it helps you to be stronger. Setting your boundaries is a form of self-care. It shows that you respect your own needs and well-being. When you respect your limits and trust your instincts, you take control of your life. You become the driver of your vehicle.

These tools can be applied in various areas of your daily life. If you feel uncomfortable around certain people, it's okay to step back. Your intuition might be telling you something important. Set limits on how much work you can handle. If you feel overwhelmed, listen to your intuition and ask for help.

Your loved ones must be informed about your boundaries. Let them know what you will and will not tolerate from them. If something doesn't feel right, trust your intuition and communicate your feelings. Your intuition will tell you when you need a break so you can take care of yourself. By understanding and respecting your limits, you create a safe and respectful space for yourself. Embracing these tools is like embarking on a journey where you're in control, making decisions that lead to personal growth, healthy relationships, and a more fulfilling life.

## 6. Living a Purpose-Driven Life

I am sure a lot of people often think about their lives and wonder why they are here on earth and what their purpose is. Some may live their lives aimlessly and pleasing others, not knowing they even exist or who they are, maybe because it is easy or they are not aware. This is like sleepwalking. You may have heard the term "unawakened one" used for such people. They are not aware.

Do you ever wonder what it is like to live a life that is meaningful? This journey is about understanding or discovering what is your life purpose. What is it that makes you or your heart feel alive? We will delve into how living a purposeful life can bring you happiness, how you can find your unique purpose, and how you can make the most of your day,

It is very rewarding to live a purposeful life. When you do so, you wake up every morning feeling excited to start your day. I know I do. I have always believed in doing what I love, working in areas that I love, or helping others, and also being indulged in creative endeavours. For me, twenty-four hours in a day is not enough; time goes by so quickly because I enjoy what I do and look forward to continuing the day or starting the next day. At the end of the day, I feel happy with my accomplishments.

When you have a clear sense of your purpose and love what you do or are doing things that align with your purpose, you feel a sense of accomplishment and contentment, which will make you feel happy.

When you do what brings you joy and brings joy to those around you, living with purpose is what gives you a reason to keep going even when things are tough.

Living with intention often involves doing things that bring joy not only to you but also to others around you. Having a sense of direction brings harmony and balance to your life. Know what you are passionate about and you can make a positive impact. Think about what you love to do. Your calling could be connected to something you enjoy. Consider your strengths and talents. How can you use them to make a difference? Doing so might involve making the world a better place, even in small ways.

We all can get so wrapped up in our daily lives that we forget to pay attention to our own needs. I recommend you take the time to listen to your heart and ask yourself what makes you feel happy and alive. Your heart knows what your purpose is before you do. It is all about making choices daily to bring you closer to your goals; it is not about a big dream.

Take a moment each day to take a step towards your goals by breaking your vision into small steps to make it easier to achieve. That will give you a sense of progress. Never give up. Even if at times things are not going the way you hope, be persistent. Even a few minutes can make a difference, and in time you will achieve your goals sooner than expected.

When I feel the task is too great and overwhelming, I quickly shift my focus from being overwhelmed to talking myself into starting the task for even five minutes or just doing one little bit of it to get myself started so I won't be hard on myself for not completing the task, because I will then have achieved getting it started. When I do start, the motivation kicks in and I do more than what I told myself I would do. Sometimes I may end up completing the task without realizing that it felt too overwhelming to start.

Then there are times I may not be able to complete the tasks but still do more than I initially decided to do. That itself is better than not getting started. I then continue at a later time and complete it. I often used this technique when I was dealing with health issues. This helped me to function in my daily life rather than letting health issues get in the way of living.

In the very same way, if you feel you have a certain purpose in your life that you wish to achieve, don't worry about not being able to achieve what you wish to do. Just concentrate on getting started, be kind to yourself, do what you can when you can, and keep going. Be persistent and consistent. You will be happy that you did.

A student of mine followed these suggestions and found them very helpful. She now feels that she can achieve more than she thought she could and feels motivated to start small—rather than avoiding anything, which leads to things not being done, which in turn leads to disappointment in herself and can spiral downward.

She was open to learning and growing and found that a simple thing such as getting started can lead to accomplishing more than expected and that the feeling of accomplishment leads to happiness.

In the same way, remember what your vision is and use the same motivation to live your purpose, and just be persistent and consistent to follow what you feel is right for you, and live your purpose. Living your purpose is a true way to live a fulfilling life.

# Chapter 5

## Change and Transformation

### 1. Constant Change

WE ALL KNOW THAT LIFE IS UNPREDICTABLE AND THAT CHANGE IS unavoidable and that we continue to go through constant change. No matter how much we hope and pray for things to remain the same, it is not possible. Some people do not like going through changes and may try to control certain life circumstances, but sadly, despite their efforts, change is inevitable. People who are not open to changes tend to be more stressed or uptight. You may even notice that they tend to become angry easily.

Be open to change. Consider life as an incredible and adventurous journey you are on, where things are always shifting and evolving. Transformation comes from the changes.

Just as a butterfly starts out as a caterpillar and then transforms into a beautiful butterfly (one of my favorite childhood stories, like the ugly duckling becoming a beautiful swan), we are always changing and growing to become better versions of ourselves. Life takes us through various experiences throughout our lives. For some of us, it may be painful and difficult, but being open to accepting our experiences with grace teaches us a great deal about truly becoming a better person. Realistically there are some exceptions to the rule, but I prefer to look on the positive side and encourage you to lean towards the positive.

If you have read my books *Take Charge: Reclaim Your Life and Be Your True Self* and *My Spiritual Journey: Life as an Empath*, you will understand the many experiences shared in those books. There was a time when I used to think that some people who have lived to be one hundred years old may not have had all these experiences.

Throughout the experiences in my life journey, I accepted all the changes that life presented me with. Some were harsh and painful. It didn't matter what the experiences were; these experiences are what made me who I am today. The experiences gave me the knowledge and wisdom to be able to do what I do today.

It is also the experiences in my life that have led me to share my stories to help others through the written words in my books.

I know there may be some people who have turned bitter because of life's experiences. It is really not their fault, because they are not yet aware or awakened. They are going through their journey. We need to have compassion for them and send them positive energies.

Allowing yourself to be accepting of the constant change helps you to grow and learn, which will help you to transform to become a better and stronger version of yourself. Each milestone in our lives is a new chapter in our story, filled with its own lessons and joys. When we learn from our experiences, we acquire the wisdom and ability to teach and help others, as I am now doing through my work as a holistic practitioner.

Some changes that we go through may be scary at first, but remember: these are chances for us to learn, grow, and discover how strong we really are. We face challenges when things shift; that is when we find our inner strength. We learn from the changes we encounter in life. Such changes could be moving to a new country, starting a new job, or moving to a new place. All of these experiences can be scary yet exciting.

We are in control of our own lives. Just like an artist, we create paintings of our choice, and each brushstroke is the experience. We are in control of how we want to paint the pictures. You are in control of your painting.

As you paint, you may decide how you want to paint, but unexpectedly you realize you don't have a certain colour, and you carry on making do with what you have and still create something beautiful. That means you didn't give up. You learned to create a new colour from what you had and continued. In life that is what we need to do—accept our circumstances and carry on to create lives for ourselves that are beautiful. I have often been open and creative to make do with what I have to create my own masterpiece not only in arts and crafts but also in life circumstances.

Change can also mean letting go of the old and making room for new and exciting things, just like a tree shedding its leaves in the fall. Sometimes the change is beyond our control and we go with it. Sometimes we need to make conscious decisions to make the change. When things are holding us back and are not making us happy, we need to make a conscious decision to change and let go of things that are holding us back or circumstances that are not good or healthy for us.

Throughout our lives, there will be changes that are beyond our control, just like my having gone through health challenges that were beyond my control. I learned to accept the challenges and did my best to not let them control my life and continued to live my life in such a way that I did not allow any challenges to stop me from reaching my goals.

I persisted and continued while I dealt with the challenges. There were also times when I made conscious decisions to make the changes to my life. I made a decision to leave a marriage that was not healthy for me. I moved to Vancouver, British

Columbia, to put my life back together and more recently relocated to Georgina, Ontario, to be closer to the water. I am transitioning from primarily being a floral designer to being a holistic practitioner because I feel I can make a positive impact on the lives of many in that role.

Even though I love being a floral designer and will always love to design, the joys I felt in the impact I made in the lives of others are far greater than the joys I felt as a designer. I will continue to design, but will do so mostly to keep me balanced as a person. I am choosing to be a holistic practitioner to feed my soul and fulfil my purpose; choosing to design occasionally feeds the other part of my soul.

It is best for us to consider change as a gift that allows us the chance to face the unknown and step into the world of possibilities. It is also a gift to liberate yourself from fears that hold you back. Teaching others to be open to change and growth is meaningful. I am always ready to embrace the unknown and accept change as it comes or make changes as I need.

I will continue to encounter change and most likely make conscious changes throughout my life as needed. I encourage you to do the same; you will be happy you did because you will have a sense of freedom from self-inflicted restrictions.

## 2. Opportunities

By being open to change and growth, you are creating opportunities for yourself to go through the transition. I have had the honour and pleasure of witnessing the transitions my students go through when they embrace change, learn to grow, and open themselves up to willingly let go of the past traumas that are preventing them from experiencing true joy and happiness.

By doing so, they open up possibilities to feel liberated and happy. They open up options for themselves to grow and become more aware of themselves, and they give themselves the gift of opportunity to grow in so many areas of their life. When things start to shift and change, there is a chance to find something amazing.

When you are open to change, you may find that your perceptions start to change. You may become more aware of your interest and true passion, and you may set new goals and work towards achieving them. These moments, when things are transitioning from one state to another, are golden opportunities waiting for us to grab.

Take advantage of options during the times of transition by being aware and recognizing them. Change is like a new door opening when one closes, bringing fresh opportunities with it. Being aware helps you to not miss the opportunities that may show up, because sometimes these doors open when you least expect it.

Such an opportunity could be you meeting someone unexpectedly and the person suddenly having an opportunity for you, such as a job you have always wanted. Or it may be the possibility of travelling to a new place. We just never know when opportunity will show up; that is why, if we are open to unexpected change, we can take advantage of the prospects presented to us, which can shape our lives in incredible ways.

Consider change as a fresh start or a beginning of a new chapter in your life, like a new chapter in a book.

We need to pause during the unique moment of transition to reflect and think about what it is we really want in our lives, and what our dreams and goals are.

Transitions can be like a roller coaster ride, full of twists and turns. Unexpectedly, you may dive so quickly you can hardly catch your breath. You will experience mixed feelings. Instead of being fearful, try to stay calm and go with the flow. You will find that the ride can feel quite thrilling.

Be open to changes that come through, and tell yourself, "I am ready for whatever comes my way!" I tend to keep my eyes wide open so I do not miss any opportunities that may come my way. I stay curious and like to explore different paths. Even when things may seem uncertain, I know that there is always a chance to discover something new or something wonderful. So I am forever ready for those unexpected moments. I am ready to expect the unexpected and accept when people are predictably unpredictable.

With transitions, you gain new skills and experiences. It is as though you are going to school for the first time to learn things you never learned before. Life itself is like a school; you learn new things every day. Life experiences are the best education you will ever have. You learn more from life experiences than you will from any school. The skills you learn from life can open doors to possibilities you would never have considered before.

I have often been like a sponge, soaking up all the knowledge and wisdom that these transitions offer. The changes and transitions that I have experienced in the past few years from the onset of the COVID-19 lockdown are something I never imagined or considered. Before the pandemic, I never imagined that someday I would have my books published, change my career, teach workshops, or even that I would adopt technology as an important part of my life.

The COVID-19 pandemic lockdown brought a lot of change to many lives. It was unexpected, but I was open and ready for whatever change came my way, and I seized the opportunities these changes brought about. I am happy to say that by being open to the changes of these unexpected situations, I embraced the opportunity to let them lead me to live the life that I feel I am meant to live. What I am currently doing now is something I thought I would like to do someday, and the lockdown helped to accelerate it and helped me to do what I have always wanted to do. I think that if I had fallen into the fear of how the pandemic could affect us negatively, I would not have been able to achieve what I have during the lockdown.

I took the opportunity during the lockdown to publish my books, overcome my fears of technology, and educate myself in the digital world. It was scary at first delving into the technical world, but I persisted and I learned, taking advantage of every opportunity that was presented to me. I was fortunate to meet Stephanie from YSpace, who opened a world of possibilities for me to learn. Even though I was scared of technology, I kept trying and gained many new skills. I know I still have a lot more to understand, and I will keep improving.

I was open to the opportunities that were offered through YSpace. I registered for every programme that was available to me. It was as if the opportunity came knocking on my door, and I was willing to open my door to let it in. This was possible because the Town of Georgina, in collaboration with York University and York Region, offers programmes to support new businesses in Georgina. There were times when opportunities knocked at my door again, but the door was stuck even though I wanted to open it. However, I was not going to let these prospects pass by just because the door was stuck. I figured out a way to let it in by opening up a window. When you do not want to let it pass, find a way to let it in.

I feel that it is so important that everyone to be willing and open to learn and make the most of the change and the chances that life presents us with. Opportunities in life are like puzzle pieces of a mysterious picture. As you start to put all the pieces together, you will be amazed when you step back and see the big picture. You may not have expected the picture to be beautiful, and it is a pleasant surprise.

Consider life as a mysterious picture. Putting the pieces together can, at times, be stressful because you may feel you do not know what to expect or how to put the pieces together. But if you persist in putting the pieces together, it is rewarding to see what unfolds. Remember: opportunities do not necessarily show up with headlights or big announcements; it is up to us to stay tuned and be aware of what comes. That is why I teach others to pay attention to all the subtle incidents, trust your gut feelings, and be aware of the changes that bring opportunity to your front doorsteps. It is like listening to the soft whisper in your mind. You will find that doors open up that you never knew existed. I know this.

## 3. Personal Growth

The Healing Journey Program is all about personal and spiritual growth. In the program, I you take on a journey to dive within yourself to look into those areas within you that you are avoiding and to prompt you to face what you may discover. Sometimes fear prevents you from seeing what you need to face and addressing it to help you to move on. Personal growth is like going on a journey of self-discovery. You start at one point, and as you travel, you discover new places and experiences. Along the way, you learn more about yourself. Life's journey is a bit like that—full of twists and turns that help you evolve and become more resilient.

In your personal growth, you start out like a tiny seed. Over time, you grow to become a tall and strong tree. You start small, with your dreams and ambitions. As you grow and take care of yourself, you start to blossom. Every step you take and the challenges that you overcome add a ring to your growth, making you stronger and wiser. The Healing Journey Program helps you to navigate through the darkness by providing you with the tools to shed light on your path, allowing you to come out of your darkness.

Personal growth is a process just like the work of a sculptor who chisels away the unnecessary pieces to reveal a masterpiece, or the peeling off the layers of an onion to get to the core. It is not always easy, just as with a sculptor who has to carefully chisel. You are uncovering your true potential or your true self. If you have read my book *Take Charge: Reclaim Your Life and Be Your True Self*, you will understand the journey of my personal growth.

Sometimes going through the process of personal growth is like wearing new shoes; it is uncomfortable at first. It is in those uncomfortable moments that growth happens. Life is like a puzzle, as mentioned earlier. It takes time to put the pieces together to reveal the beautiful picture. Learn to be persistent through the process of putting it together. Before you start putting the pieces together, it's a pile of little pieces that do not make sense.

In the Healing Journey Program, individuals are helped through gentle encouragement to take their time and be patient as they piece together their personal growth just as if they are delicately restoring a broken piece of pottery. Despite the visible imperfections and the challenge of mending tiny, irreparable pieces, they are guided in piecing together the fragments of their lives, much like broken piece of pottery. With care and a touch of gold, the reassembled whole becomes a beautiful work of art, shimmering where the pieces unite.

The art of restoring broken pottery with gold, highlighting the cracks, is called Kintsugi (also known as Kintsukuroi). This traditional Japanese technique involves mending the broken pieces of pottery with lacquer mixed with powdered gold, silver, or platinum. It is about embracing flaws and imperfection. Personal growth and spiritual growth are very much like that. When you mend your broken pieces together, you are creating a beautiful new you with your true self intact. The true shape of the pottery does not change once reassembled. I have clients who have written their stories about their personal and spiritual growth and the transformations they have experienced in my book *My Spiritual Journey: Life as an Empath*.

M clients are provided with tools and know-how to let go of past traumas and not let it affect them in their daily lives, which helps them to let go of anger and watch what goes on around them without letting it affect them. We always do updates when we start sessions on the progress they have made before we proceed.

One of these updates I recently received from my client was "My HS (high school) reunion is fast approaching, and my other committee organizers are already getting on each other's nerves. I guess I'm happy that I'm not being affected and I get to referee them to be able to work together. I get to be able to look at them and even laugh a bit at the way they're acting. The fact that I don't get sucked up in their drama—I feel that's a big accomplishment for me."

When we carry anger inside, we feel agitated all the time. When there is negativity in a situation, we will act out with irritation. However, when we are at peace within, we learn to have the ability to create our shield, keeping us in our bubble that protects us from being affected by the drama around us.

While working around those who feel constant stress and are expressing their stress, I have my bubble I stay within, and I am not bothered by it as it does not belong to me. I was even told that I could ignore all of that and stay calm.

I heard comments like "Jacinta is in her Zen space," and then I was asked, "Do you meditate a lot or all the time to be in your Zen space?" My response to that was "I do not need to meditate to be Zen; I choose to be in my Zen space." You, too, can choose to be in your Zen space as well. At first it may take some effort to practise, but in time it can become your second nature.

## 4. Letting Go

The key to healing is to let go of the past that does not serve you. If you do not, you will feel as if you are carrying very heavy baggage around. In time, you could hurt yourself as well as burn yourself out. You alone have the power to put the bags down and move forward. No one can take the bags off you if you do not let it go. When you finally let go of your bags, you can freely walk to a future filled with amazing possibilities. I would like to walk you through this transformative journey of letting go of the past and allowing yourself to walk into a future that is bright and awaits you.

Releasing the past means turning your focus towards the future. One of the key things that I do to help people in the Healing Journey Program is to start by getting them to unlock the baggage they have been carrying all their lives. Most of this baggage is very heavy and painful, which in time weighs them, down making it difficult for them to move forward. I help them to toss out all unnecessary heavy items that are weighing them down.

When you lose your baggage, you can feel relief, feel free, fly like a bird, and soar as high as you wish. It is like purging and cleaning out your wardrobe and getting rid of clothes that no longer fit you and are taking up space, which makes it difficult to add new outfits. Shedding the past is like letting go of what no longer fits you so you can create space for new experiences and new opportunities, or to allow new relationships to come into your life.

Consider your life as a collection of books. Each phase of your life is a chapter that is a story. Each book is a story from the past. Once that story is written and read, you cannot change it. However, you can write a new book. Let the past go, and start fresh. Start a new story from the beginning, and see how it unfolds. You have new pages to start your own story. You are the author of your book, shaping it with every decision you make.

I published two books prior to this one. Although I started out to write this book two years ago, I was not able to complete it then, as I was still writing the story in my life. I knew what to write about, but in order to complete my book, I needed time and experience to gain the material to be put into words.

Yes, we can have some plans or goals we can set for ourselves and reach for. In order to reach our goals, we need to let go of the past that serves no purpose any longer. Not only do we release the past that no longer serves us, but we should also not allow anything that does not serve us to get in the way of us reaching our goals. Once again, I am stressing the importance of being persistent and consistent in what we want to achieve.

At times, letting go may be hard, but we must persist to try till we succeed.

In my observation, when people hold on to grudges or have regrets, they are often angrier than those who generally are free of any grudges. I do not believe in holding a grudge or believe in having regrets. If I feel I have been wronged by anyone, I simply address it with that person. I express my thoughts and clear the issues. There are times when people may unintentionally behave in an upsetting manner, so clearing the air helps to achieve better understanding.

However, there are times when people may just be intentionally hurtful. Then it is still best to express your feelings and get past it and set your boundary. You may have to consider detaching yourself from people that are toxic and moving on. By doing this, you are allowing yourself to free yourself from holding on to any grudge that is not healthy for you.

Regret is something I feel we must consciously decide not to hold on to. People often feel regret about something they may have done or may not have done. If you feel you have any regrets, ask yourself why. Then consider the fact that when you made the decision about the situation, it was right at the time because you didn't know what you know now. Be kind to yourself and let go of the regret that is holding you back or hurting you, because you know that you can never turn the clock back and undo anything that has happened.

Letting go of grudges and regrets helps you to feel liberated and light and not hold on to things that are dragging you down. When you do so, you will also notice that you don't feel angered as easily. By moving forward, you focus on what is ahead of you and allow yourself to move towards endless opportunities ahead of you and create for yourself a fulfilling future. This will lead to you feeling happier.

I have witnessed clients who were eager to grow and to learn how to be free of the past and accept the change and transformation. In doing so, they feel so much lighter and happier—so much so that people they encounter regularly comment on their demeanours and how they look lighter and so happy that they glow. These clients attribute this to the Healing Journey Program they embarked on.

## 5. Trusting Your Heart

Your heart is your compass to your true self. Your heart guides you to what truly aligns with you and your values. Consider your heart as your true friend who knows and wants what is best for you. Your heart knows you better than anyone in the world, including yourself. When you are going through the stages of your growth and transformation, your heart will guide you and nudge you towards the right direction.

Trusting your heart leads you towards the inner wisdom that will guide you through paths you have not taken. When you trust your heart and pay attention to the inner voice that is speaking to you, you will know whether decisions feel right for you or not. That is why you must stay tuned in to those subtle nudges that you feel.

Most times, our inner voices will be very subtle; therefore, we must learn to pay attention. Oftentimes we let our minds talk us out of these nudges. I know I did that myself because of my logical mind. I learned over the years to trust my inner voice when I listened.

Tuning in to your heart is a bit like tuning in to your soul. In times of change, your heart gives you messages that resonate with your true self. These are like intuitive signals that guide you towards what feels right. With practise you will eventually notice that the subtle voices do get louder, and you will learn to trust them. When you continually practise tuning in for guidance, it becomes a natural part of you, and you eventually will not need to make a conscious effort to do so. This is what it is like for me. I do not need to think or meditate to hear what my guidance wants to tell me. I am attuned naturally. I feel that inner voice through a sensation I feel in my body; then I hear it in my mind's ear.

There were times in your life when you had to make decisions and were afraid that you would make the wrong ones and avoided them. For example, perhaps someone told you of a new job opportunity that would be really great for you, but you were afraid to take action and apply for the job because you were not sure you would get it or that it would be right for you. You ended up letting an opportunity pass you by.

Learn to tune in to your heart for guidance when an opportunity knocks. Go within and listen to what your guidance tells you. If it is a good opportunity, you will sense and feel that it feels right for you. When something is not right for you, you will sense a feeling of discomfort. I sense discomfort in my heart when things are not right for me. The feeling is like a palpitation or even difficulty in breathing if it is really bad.

When people ask me about situations they are hoping will have a positive outcome, they wonder whether my guidance and help can predict what that outcome may be. Interestingly, when that question is asked of me, a smile forms on my face, and I feel a genuine joy and happiness in my heart that I suddenly feel from out of the blue. Soon I find out that the person asking the question has received the positive result he or she has been hoping for.

I say tune in to your heart for guidance, because in my experience that is what I have done, and I feel it in my body, starting from my heart, just as I have mentioned. When something is not positive, I feel my heart start to palpitate, have difficulty breathing, and feel anxiety. If something is positive, I feel joy swell from my heart to form a smile on my face.

Perhaps you may feel such things in ways similar to how I do, or you may have a different type of sensation. By paying close attention to your body's sensations, you will learn how your body will communicate with you, and with practise you can learn to trust your heart and your inner guidance to help you with any decisions you need to make in your life that will be right for you.

By listening to your heart, your growth and transformation become easy. You gain confidence in all aspects of your life, especially in making decisions. Others will notice your growth and that you carry yourself with confidence. There will be a glow about you that people will notice in you.

You will start to inspire others through your transformation, and people will feel inspired. I know this to be true because my students enrolled in the Healing Journey Program continue to tell me about how people around them notice the transformation and growth in them, that they are glowing, and how confident and inspiring they are.

Remember that your heart is your true friend. It is the loudest when you are going through the changes. It will guide you through thick and thin, and you can always rely on it to guide you in the right direction. It may not always be easy, but it will be right for you.

Things that are good for you are not always easy, but if you embrace your change and growth with open arms, it gets a lot easier. It is tough when you resist it. Your heart will help you be more in tune with your values. Trust its nudges and its gentle tugs.

## 6. Resilience and Positivity

Embracing change helps the transformation go much easier. You will also notice or become more aware that life is full of surprises whether you expect them or not. Change does not have to be scary or overwhelming. Practise having a positive outlook and trusting your heart's guidance. In this way, you will manage to overcome life's challenges with grace and confidence.

Let's go through how you can arm yourself with the skills and power of resilience and positivity. Think of resilience as your protective shield to protect yourself, just as soldiers in the olden days wore suits of armour to protect themselves. Having resilience is what helps you to face challenges and bounce back. It helps you to withstand the impact of the change. You become stronger after you go through rough experiences in life.

Resilience is like a muscle. The more you exercise it, the more you build up its strength. When you encounter change or challenges, you can face them head-on.

I have a big, beautiful willow tree in my backyard that looks like a hundred-year-old tree. When the strong wind blows, the branches sway with the wind. The wind may bend its branches, but it doesn't break, That's resilience in action. When you embrace change, you become the willow that can sway with the challenges without losing your core strength,

Resilience is about having the ability to adapt to changes. As you all know, life is like the weather, which can vary between sunshine, rain, storms, and lightning. Being resilient is like being prepared for the weather accordingly. You adjust to weather conditions, being prepared with an umbrella when it rains or a warm coat when it's cold. The ability to adapt accordingly helps you to find a way to thrive in all situations. You adjust and find new ways to shine, no matter what comes your way.

Life experiences have taught me to be resilient, and now I help others to be resilient. You, too, can adapt and find new ways to shine.

Oftentimes we hear people encouraging each other about being positive. Positivity is not about ignoring challenges or pretending that everything is fine and dandy. It is more about not dwelling on a problem so much that it takes you to a dark hole, having an optimistic approach, and dealing with the problem by seeking a solution that will help you resolve any issues you are dealing with.

Positivity is like a bright light that helps guide you out of the darkness. It is about focusing on the good things and on the lessons challenges bring to help you with your growth. Having a positive outlook is like wearing a pair of glasses to help you with your vision. With a positive outlook, you see the world in a different light.

Being optimistic helps you to see things from different perspectives. When change happens, you can choose to put on these glasses and look for the good. You can search for the positive aspects in every situation. Positivity is a bit like a treasure hunt; you uncover the gems of hope and optimism that are often hidden beneath the surface.

I have a client who came to Canada to visit her friend. When we met, she decided to enrol in the Healing Journey Program and extended her stay. She worked hard on her personal growth and started to feel happier and calmer. She was concerned that when she returned home, she might fall back into the same state she was in.

She was assured that the work she invests in her personal growth stays with her no matter where she goes because she has developed a new perception of life. How she sees life's situations, how she hears what is communicated to her, and how she thinks all changes, and the new-found happiness and calmness stay with her no matter where she goes or where she is.

Upon her return home, she continued with the healing journey to continue with her growth, as she still had a lot more to learn and grow. She continued diligently making the effort to learn. Now she is in a good place because all that she has learned has been ingrained and has become a part of her.

When I see growth in others who have worked so hard to reach their happy places, it brings me so much joy over and over again with each person I work with. It is a beautiful feeling to witness so much joy and happiness in others.

When you embrace change with positivity, you are allowing yourself to open yourself to new possibilities and new beginnings. It is advisable to start the day with the affirmation "Today is a good day and I intend to make it a good day." When you say this affirmation, you become more aware of ensuring that you will do your best to stay positive and prevent yourself from allowing any negativity to indulge in your day. Positivity is like a compass that points you towards the beauty and potential that change can bring.

A bright outlook is also a mindset that you want to have. Instead of dwelling on what's wrong with your life, you shift your focus to what's possible and what you can learn.

As you journey through life's challenges, remember that you have the power of resilience and positivity—skills that will help you to shape your life in how you want to live your life. Reach for your goals, and fill them with endless possibilities.

## Chapter 6

*Universal Love*

## 1. Many Facets of Love

LOVE IS UNIVERSAL. THE VARIOUS EMOTIONS, BEHAVIOURS, AND experiences surrounding this topic are very complex and difficult to explain with a single definition. We all experience different forms of love from the time we are born. Mothers love, we receive love from family and friends, and we experience love with romantic partners. Love is such a powerful energy; it has the power to heal as well as hurt greatly.

For centuries, we have heard so many stories of how love has been impactful both positively and negatively. I say "negatively" because there are some instances when some actions people have taken in the name of love have been very destructive. I would like us to reveal the significance of the various forms of expression of love in human relationships among family, friends, and society.

There are several distinctive types of love. Each type has its own unique characteristics. There are many movies and books written about romantic love. It involves intense emotional interaction or connection between two people, usually accompanied by the desire for companionship or physical attraction, which people refer to as having chemistry between them.

Love is not only about romantic love; it is also about the bond between friends or between parents and children. This love between parents and children or amongst close friends is an expression of emotion characterized by support, a deep sense of responsibility for each other, and unconditional care.

Strong connections between friendships that are cherished are important aspects of love. These types of bonds offer a safe space and comfort for sharing experiences and thoughts. This bond requires nurturing and caring for the friendship to flourish. Love isn't just about people, though. It's also about how we care for animals, plants, and the world around us. It shows how we're all connected and why it's important to take care of our planet. More and more people now consider animals as family members. People consider their pets as their children.

Love is expressed in many different ways. Showing compassion to others, acts of kindness, offering to lend a helping hand, and gestures of selflessness are all examples of love. Love is not about making grand gestures; it can be as simple as comforting someone in a time of distress or being a shoulder for someone to cry on. These small gestures show the presence of love. Meaningful connections are developed through these genuine interactions.

Different people express love differently. Some express love through their actions, while others are vocal and verbal by saying "I love you." Oftentimes people mistake nonverbal expression as a lack of love. To avoid misunderstanding, it is important for couples that are together to learn how they express their love for each other.

Women in general are known to be more expressive about their love for their spouses or partners and can feel unloved if they are with partners or spouses who are not the type to express their love vocally. When couples are not consciously aware of the way they communicate, one or the other person in the couple can mistakenly feel that his or her partner does not care or love him or her any more, which leads to strain in their relationship.

However, if they are aware, then there are fewer chances of such misunderstanding.

It is wise to share openly from your heart when you are meeting a potential partner to express that you may or may not be a vocal person. State that if you do no not say "I love you" habitually, it does not mean you do not care or love your partner. And if you are vocal and like to hear love expressed vocally, you may consider sharing how hearing those words makes you feel loved and comforted.

When this is shared openly, then the couple may make the effort to express love vocally sometimes so both partners feel loved. The partners might consider making the effort to understand that if they do not hear those loving words, they need not be upset or feel unloved but could look at the actions of love shown by their partners to feel the security of love.

Nonverbal cues of love—such as a simple smile, a hug, and meaningful glances—can be powerful expressions of love that help others to feel comfort and reassurance in a way words sometimes cannot.

Love is not always easy, especially when someone is going through heavy emotions, such as when there are disagreements, misunderstandings, and conflicts. This is a natural aspect of any relationship, whether it is a relationship between romantic partners, family, or friends. Working through these tough moments helps deepen the bond between each relationship.

I express myself through my actions, but I realize that some people prefer to hear the words, and I am not speaking of romantic relationships. I now have learned to be a bit more expressive verbally. It wasn't easy at first because it felt awkward. I used to think in my mind, "Why is it necessary to be vocal about it?" I showed love through my actions. But now I have made it a habit to express love vocally and am now comfortable doing so.

Love is a driving force; it has tremendous power to create positive change. Acts of kindness have the potential to create ripple effects. Conduct your life with unconditional love for others, and have the passion to show how love can have a great impact on bringing about change and happiness. See the impact and the transformation the energy of love has made.

Reiki is a universal energy life force, a healing energy also considered to be the energy of love. When you guide others with love from your heart that you feel for their well-being, combined with reiki and the energy of love, people feel calm and focused while working through healing their own traumas to become more self-aware, leading to the path of happiness.

Love's impact is felt not only in personal relationships but also within the community and society at large. It brings about positive change in the community. I live in Georgina, Ontario, in a community where people come together to support each other. We have a Facebook group, where people post to request support. No matter what the request is, responses to support the person who requested support come flooding in. People reach out to help, and those who may not be able to help refer them to where they can get help. The responses are so kind, nonjudgemental, and, most of all, very *loving*. When communities come together to support those in need, the collective expression of love can lead to impactful transformations.

People are so thoughtful and caring. It sure is a good feeling to know that the people around you have the same values and compassion for each other. Acts of love and kindness have the potential to create a ripple effect to inspire others to pay it forward.

Love finds its way through cultures and religions, touching every corner of our lives. Back in my school days at a Catholic missionary school, the teachings about love, kindness, and empathy left an impact on me. They echoed phrases like "love thy neighbour as yourself," "help those in need," and "treat others how you'd like to be treated."

The nuns were my real-life heroes, their selfless devotion inspiring a deep longing within me to follow in their footsteps. But life had its own plans, steering me towards an arranged marriage to a husband chosen by my parents. Just before my wedding, Sister Elfreda D'souza, whose wisdom I cherished, sent me a heartfelt letter: "Jacinta, you wanted to be a nun because you want to help others. You can still help even if you are not a nun."

Love isn't just an abstract concept; it's a force that shapes our mental and physical well-being. It's the key to happiness, a balm that soothes stress, and a motivator for contentment. Love heals wounds and builds unbreakable bonds, creating spaces where people feel safe to grow and change. I've learned to face life's trials with love as my guide; it's the most powerful tool in navigating life's unpredictable journey.

Understanding and accepting different forms of love can enrich and strengthen our relationships, encourage empathy, and contribute to a more compassionate and interconnected world. So let us cherish the many levels of love and allow its radiant light to shine along our paths.

## 2. Healing through Love

I truly believe that love is an incredible force in our lives. It's not just something we see in movies; it has this amazing ability to heal and transform us deeply. Love can mend emotional scars, ease pain, and bring a sense of renewal to our spirits. It goes beyond the romantic idea; it's a powerful force that guides us towards healing and wholeness.

One of the ways I work with healing is through reiki. It's all about tapping into the energy of love and channelling energies from the universe. Love, in this context, is about accepting ourselves and others completely and unconditionally. This self-acceptance is crucial for healing and creating safe spaces where we can confront our challenges and vulnerabilities without any judgement. My clients often express that they feel safe, supported, and, most of all, loved.

For me, the journey of healing starts with self-awareness, self-acceptance, and self-love. When we learn to love and accept ourselves, it generates a sense of self-respect and helps us set healthy boundaries, allowing us to stay true to who we are.

In relationships, love acts like a soothing balm for emotional wounds. When we face heartbreak, betrayal, or loss, the support and understanding of loved ones can ease the pain and bring comfort. Sharing our struggles and vulnerabilities with trusted friends or family can release pent-up emotions. When we are surrounded by people who are kind and caring, it helps speed up healing, allowing us to process our emotions in order for us to recover.

In romantic relationships, when partners' commitment and support of each other can be sources of healing when one is going through a rough patch in life, regarding challenges with health or any other difficulties they may experience together. When there is mutual love, they are able to draw on this love to get through life's challenges together.

Our loved ones provide a safe space where we can show our vulnerabilities and find peace. Being vulnerable can be incredibly healing itself, opening doors to understanding, empathy, and personal growth. Love in partnerships encourages emotional intimacy and open communication, which are foundations of healthy relationships and partnerships.

People express love in various therapeutic methods. Some express themselves through music, art, or poetry. I am sure you are already familiar with how people express love through songs. A person who may not be skilled in verbalizing may choose a song for his or her loved one to express love. Some may even listen to music of love to heal.

Self-compassion is also a big part of love. It is a priority to treat ourselves with kindness and understanding, just as we would a friend, creating a space for personal growth. This involves acknowledging our pain, embracing imperfections, and fostering inner warmth. This practice counters negative self-talk, reduces shame, and builds emotional strength, aiding in the healing journey.

In times of trauma, love becomes a beacon of hope and resilience. My clients and students who are enrolled in the Healing Journey Program are guided by me to dive deep within and love every part of themselves so they can heal the traumas they have experienced in their lives. Love has the ability to bring people together and inspire positivity, which is instrumental in healing.

Love's ability to heal is undeniable. When we open our hearts and show kindness and love unto others, it brings about harmony and unity. Whether in personal relationships, self-care practices, or broader community contexts, love has the power to heal wounds, soothe pain, and nurture our hearts and souls. As we accept the healing potential of love, we learn to have more understanding, empathy, and overall well-being, both for ourselves and for everyone around us.

## 3. Self-Love and Self-Care

Being a natural caregiver, self-love and self-care weren't on my radar back when I was responsible for taking care of my in-laws. Life's challenges led me through a whirlwind of change and growth. Through deep self-reflection, I began to understand my own needs and desires. I've always had a passion for helping others, sometimes forgetting to prioritize my well-being.

While giving so much, I started feeling taken for granted. Life's demands often overshadowed the importance of caring for myself. Feeling unappreciated was a tough experience.

I knew I needed a change without compromising my values. It was time to reassess my life and find happiness while staying true to my compassionate nature. That's when I realized the importance of my mental and emotional well-being.

Putting myself first felt like a radical shift. But I learned that when I'm emotionally and mentally in a good place, I'm better equipped to support others. Setting healthy boundaries and saying no to those who took advantage of my kindness became crucial.

Self-love became a priority for my well-being. It meant treating myself with kindness, understanding, and compassion— the same way I treated others. Accepting my flaws and valuing my uniqueness were key parts of this journey.

Forgiving myself for past mistakes was crucial. Accepting my humanity allowed me to let go of guilt and shame, focusing instead on learning and growing.

I made sure to make self-care intentional so I would not forget to care for myself first. I realized that neglecting myself only blocked my ability to help others effectively. It wasn't selfish; it was a way for me to recharge so I could continue supporting others.

Taking care of my body through healthy meals, exercise, and rest became a conscious choice and priority. Emotional self-care involved sharing feelings with a supportive network and engaging in activities that brought me joy.

Creativity became my mental self-care outlet. Singing and crafting helped me express myself and recharge after mentally exhausting workshops. Balancing my time and setting boundaries became crucial to prevent burnout. I find that when I indulge in anything creative, I feel refreshed and rejuvenated, especially after working on projects that require the exertion of mental power.

Prioritizing my well-being showed my commitment to my own happiness. Creating a personalized routine that included walks, hobbies, and self-care rituals became a powerful way to integrate self-love into my life. I may be exhausted physically, but when I engage myself in creative activity, I feel energized mentally as well as physically. Learn about your self-care needs and act upon them. You will feel more energized.

Seeking professional help when needed was part of this journey. Whether through acupuncture, therapy, or seeking medical advice, it was a proactive step towards self-love. When I feel drained or unwell, I get acupuncture treatments and chiropractic treatments so I can bounce back and feel more energized to function well.

By being kind to myself, I hoped to inspire others to prioritize their well-being. Self-love allowed me to offer genuine care to others and become a source of support and resilience. Nurturing self-love and practising self-care have become vital to me for a balanced and fulfilling life. By taking care of ourselves, we demonstrate to others the importance of self-care and inspire a culture of compassion and vitality.

## 4. Loving Relationships

Creating loving relationships is deeply tied to our perspectives on life. If you naturally see the positive side, building loving connections feels natural. People who radiate positivity often are loving, giving, and kind. It's no surprise that others are drawn to those who are approachable and friendly.

When we develop loving relationships, it is like a shared journey of growth, respect, and shared experiences. It's about opening up the power of empathy and effective communication, and investing time and effort into bonds that are meaningful to our lives.

Empathy is the heart of meaningful relationships. It's about stepping into someone else's shoes, feeling what that person feels, and truly understanding his or her perspective. When we show genuine interest and listen actively, we create a space of acceptance in which people feel seen and valued for who they are. I often tell others to try and step into others' shoes so they can understand them better. This is something I do to understand others. More often than not, I can feel what others feel because I am an empath, although my brain does often guide me to step into others' shoes to understand situations better.

Clear and open communication is important for nurturing loving relationships. Sharing thoughts and feelings builds a strong connection that goes beyond barriers. Honest conversations lead the way for understanding and prevent misunderstandings. I am very honest and at times am considered to be brutally honest in the way I get my message across. People value and appreciate my honesty even though it may be painful. They know I mean well and accept it gracefully.

Choosing words thoughtfully and speaking honestly is what fuels relationship growth. Expressing gratitude and addressing conflicts with sensitivity strengthens bonds and develops deeper understanding. Investing time and effort is crucial. Quality time together builds memories and strengthens emotional ties. Supporting each other's growth and celebrating achievements cultivates a sense of togetherness. I strongly believe in prioritizing my family, friends, and the people I know over monetary gain.

Respect is the foundation. Treating others with consideration, valuing opinions, and respecting boundaries encourages mutual respect. Learning to respect ourselves is key; it naturally extends to respecting others. Establishing healthy boundaries maintains balance and preserves well-being. It ensures that relationships remain respectful and beneficial for both parties.

Small acts of kindness show love and appreciation. Whether it's cooking a meal or offering support, these gestures warm the heart and strengthen connections. Physical touches, such as hugs, create a comforting bond. These acts remind us of our emotional connection and provide a sense of security. I grew up in a culture where hugging is not the norm; it is something I learned over time. Forgiveness is essential. No relationship is perfect, and accepting imperfections builds healthy relationships.

Viewing conflicts as chances to grow together strengthens unity, while shared values and mutual understanding simplify relationships. My friends tell me that friendship with me is easy because they feel accepted by me without judgement and communicate honestly. Avoiding the truth can lead to misunderstandings and strained relationships.

Expressing gratitude reinforces bonds. Small gestures of appreciation go a long way in nurturing loving connections. Cultivating loving relationships is a journey of empathy, communication, time, respect, kindness, resilience, and appreciation.

## 5. Love's Power

I believe in the power of prayers and the power of love. Regardless of gender or colour or race, everyone goes through different emotions. Love is a profound and universal emotion. It has the ability to heal, connect, inspire, and uplift. There are different types of love: self-love, romantic love, love between family members, and the bonds of friendship. Love is what drives our lives and sparks our aspirations. It plays a significant role in our emotional well-being.

The presence of love in one's life contributes to increased feelings of happiness, contentment, and overall life satisfaction. Sometimes even just knowing someone cares or loves us also makes us feel wanted, which helps raise one's self-confidence and comfort, especially if we have experienced trauma in life regarding parents who are incapable of showing love and support.

When someone feels loved and supported, that person feels he or she has the strength to face life's challenges, because the loving support acts as a cushion during difficult times. It helps to feel positive rather than to feel helpless and hopeless.

Love has the ability to infuse energies to motivate us. We are driven by love both in things we care about and in creative ventures. Love for art, music, crafts, and writing are all examples of how love for something motivates each person to do something he or she loves. It also brings people together. It serves as a bonding agent. Love is accepting and nonjudgemental. It is blind to racial or cultural background.

Love is like a spark that starts a fire in us. It helps people to stay focused and work hard. An example of this is that when a person is trying to reach for a goal he or she loves, the person will work hard and be dedicated to reaching the goal. It is that love that drives the person to keep going even when things are tough. Another example of this is when a person in a toxic relationship wants to be free from all the toxicity and his or her love for freedom from such an environment will motivate the person to work towards setting himself or herself free from such an unhealthy situation. Taking the steps may seem daunting and hard, but the desire or love for freedom will fuel the fire in the person to work hard to achieve that freedom. You must also remember there were times when you felt eager to do things when you felt supported and loved. When we feel love, we are willing to show care and support well.

I have the pleasure of meeting couples that have such deep love for each other that they would do anything for each other and support each other. I live and breathe love in my life. I have enough love for everyone that I come in contact with. Sometimes I am asked, "How do you do it? How can you be so caring and loving towards people that hurt you?"

In my opinion, those who hurt others are the very people who need more love. I have experienced people growing and changing because I choose to be loving and kind no matter what others' actions towards me are. In time those people do change and grow, and they learn to be more loving as well. Love heals.

You likely have heard countless stories of people who have dedicated their lives to causes fuelled by love. As I mentioned earlier, I was impressed by the life of Mother Theresa, who dedicated her life to God and spent her life spreading love, care, and support. Her love to serve God is what fuelled her to live life the way she did. Her commitment and tireless efforts are solid proof that love can inspire us to create lasting change and make the world a better place,

Love pushes us to become better and do our best, making us think about ourselves, our actions, and how we can improve. When we care about ourselves, we start a journey to learn more about who we are, find our good qualities, and see where we can get better.

Having people who love us is like having mirrors around. They show us what we're good at and where we can do better. When they give us advice and support, we learn more about how we act, what we think, and what we do. This helps us grow and understand ourselves better.

When we do things with love, like being kind and giving, it can start a chain reaction. Other people see what we're doing and want to do good things too. This can inspire people to work together to solve problems in our society and make things better. Its power to make things better, bring people together, give us ideas, and help us all become better people shows how amazing it is.

When we realize how much love can make us feel good, help us get along with others, and even make the whole world better, we learn something important: love is what brings us all together, shows us the way, and leaves a mark that lasts a long time. When we do things with love—whether big or small—we make the world a kinder and closer place, thanks to the amazing and lasting effects of love's power to bring about change.

## 6. Love Triumphs

Love is a beautiful feeling that brings people closer and makes the world a better place. However, sometimes we face obstacles and fears that prevent us from fully experiencing and sharing love. I would like to share how we can overcome these challenges and accept love in our lives.

The fear of getting hurt is one of the more common factors that causes people to build walls around their hearts. I have been guilty of this myself. When I left an unhealthy marriage, I had a thick wall—a friend called it a steel wall—that was hard to penetrate. It remained up for only a short while because I knew that it was very unbecoming of me. For me, fear was not the reason for this wall. For me, it was more about needing the time to find who I really am. I knew back then that I did not want to be someone who did not feel emotion or love because she had allowed logic to take over.

It is not very easy to feel emotions or feel love when we are logical, but mind you, even though I may have been logical, I knew I was still kind. But I didn't allow myself to feel emotions, because I needed to be strong to deal with life at the time. People often think I am fearless, but in reality, that is not true. I feel fear too, just like everyone else, but I work at overcoming whatever fears I may experience in various situations.

It is very common for most to build barriers for fear of getting hurt. When we put up barriers or walls around us, we are preventing ourselves from getting hurt, but we are also preventing love from coming in. People put up barriers due to past experiences. Therefore, it is important that we learn to let go of the past, overcome fear, and not build a wall, so we can experience the joys and happiness love brings into our lives.

First, we need to learn to identify our fears and where they stem from, or why they exist, in order for us to know how to work on overcoming them. One of the main things that I like to help my clients with is guiding them to identify their fears. Sometimes it is easy, and sometimes it is not. In the latter case, I guide them to dive even deeper so they can identify the cause of their fear that is preventing them from letting go of the walls they have built for themselves.

In some cases, I have seen how their fears have debilitated them to the point that they cannot move forward or take action towards their growth and feel happiness. They often give fear the power to paralyze them. I encourage people to allow themselves to let go of their fears so they won't feel restricted from moving forward in life and achieving their goals.

The ability to let go of fear also boosts self-confidence. When we believe in ourselves and are aware of our own selves by believing in our worthiness and letting go of fear, we are then able to allow love to enter our lives. The Healing Journey Program is designed to help people let go of fear and cultivate self-love, which results in self-confidence, self-respect, and the building of healthy boundaries, which ripples into accepting and respecting others and developing, understanding, and loving, which help dissolve anger and resentments in relationships around them. Boosting our self-confidence is key to breaking down barriers to love. By believing in ourselves and our worthiness of love, we empower ourselves to let love into our lives.

Effective communication helps us express our feelings and concerns. When we openly share our thoughts with our loved ones, we create an environment of understanding and empathy, which can dissolve barriers and strengthen the bond of love. This motivated me to write this book to encourage you to have your voice and speak your truth from your heart.

We all hesitate to speak from our hearts for fear of being misunderstood, judged, or even disliked. Sadly, in doing so, we lose who we truly are, and misunderstandings do arise in our efforts to avoid misunderstanding.

It is important to be honest. Being honest is crucial, as it relies on trust, which serves as the foundation for any loving relationship. In new relationships, understanding each other's intentions takes time, and trust gradually builds as confidence grows in each other's genuine commitment.

Fear of rejection is another factor that holds us back from

expressing our love. It's important to remember that not every situation will lead to the outcome we desire. By accepting the possibility of rejection, we free ourselves to take risks and find genuine love. Past hurts can create emotional walls that prevent our ability to love. Seeking healing through therapy, self-reflection, and forgiveness can help us let go of these burdens, or baggage, and make space for love to grow.

Love often requires us to step outside our comfort zones. Taking small steps towards vulnerability and new experiences can gradually diminish our fears and expand our capacity for love. By overcoming and recognizing our fears, communicating openly, building trust, and healing from past wounds, we can break down the walls we build and create meaningful connections filled with love and understanding. Clients that go through these processes while on the healing journey grow in leaps and bounds. They feel happier and calmer, they release the need for control of things they cannot control, and they feel more accepting of what life has to offer.

*Chapter 7*

*Self-Discovery*

## 1. Your Heart and Soul

THE HEALING JOURNEY IS ABOUT SELF-DISCOVERY AND SELF-awareness. Imagine going on a journey to find who you are within yourself—a journey to discover the deepest part of you. I help you to take down the walls layer by layer, as if peeling off the layers of an onion, to get to the core, or depths, of your heart and soul. It is a path that anyone, regardless of language, gender or background can take to understand themselves better and find profound meaning in their life.

This is a path that anyone can take, no matter where one is in life, and no matter one's age. People have the misconception that once you reach a certain age, you cannot change. I have worked with clients doing the Healing Journey Program, who were well over fifty years of age and felt the need to change things in life so they could find their way to happiness. With hard work and commitment to their personal growth, they learned to use the tools provided to them to achieve their goals to overcome fears, gain confidence, and build healthy boundaries.

The heart often symbolizes the centre of our emotions. It is where we experience love, joy, sadness, and many other feelings. Exploring your heart means becoming attuned to your emotions and understanding how they shape your perceptions and actions. I encourage you to take time to reflect on moments that have touched your heart deeply. These could be memories of laughter with loved ones, acts of kindness you've witnessed, or even moments of personal triumph. By remembering these experiences, you can begin to understand yourself and your emotions.

Understanding your heart means getting comfortable with your vulnerabilities. It's about recognizing those emotional soft spots that make you who you are. Embracing imperfections and learning from tough times—that's where you get in touch with your heart. And then our journey moves from the heart to the soul. Your soul? It's like the core of who you are, way beyond just your physical self. It's where your passions, values, and the things that drive you reside.

Now let us move from the heart to the soul. The soul is often considered the essence of who you are, your innermost self that goes beyond the physical body. It is the source of your passions, values, and purpose in life.

To discover your soul, you may want to go on a path of self-reflection. Consider the activities that make you lose track of time, the things or interests you are passionate about. These are often indicators of what resonates deeply with your soul. Whether it's painting, playing music, helping others, or engaging in a particular profession, these passions are windows into your true self. My passion is being creative through arts or crafts or whatever it is that entails creativity. Do you know what your passions are?

Sometimes people end up living lives that everyone else expects of them. They're so busy trying to keep everyone happy that they forget what they truly want and what makes them happy. And then there are those who know their passion but feel stuck, thinking they have to spend their days taking care of others to keep the peace. If you're unsure, it might be time for some soul-searching. And if you do know, it's about time to start chasing after what you love.

Your values are a big part of this soul-searching journey. Think about the principles that guide your choices. Are you all about compassion, honesty, or creativity? Knowing your core values gives you a peek into what really makes you, you. Finding your purpose is also a big piece of this puzzle. What do you want to bring to the table? What legacy do you want to leave behind?

To find your purpose, start by practising mindfulness and self-awareness. Pay attention to how your feelings and passions mesh. Are you living according to your values? Are you taking care of your heart and soul by practising self-care and expressing yourself? And don't forget that surrounding yourself with those who support your journey of self-discovery makes a world of difference. Hang out with people who support you and encourage you to be the real you—your authentic self.

When you dive into your emotions, passions, values, and purpose, you discover these hidden gems that make you one of a kind. And as you keep examining yourself, remember: it's not about reaching some fixed destination; it's about always learning and growing.

Accept the tough moments and celebrate those victories, because every step adds up to this beautiful story that's your life. Your heart and soul are like guides steering you towards a genuine, joyful life that's deeply connected to yourself and the world. I firmly believe in staying open to learning. No matter our age or how much we know, there's always something new to discover.

## 2. Purpose in Life

Have you ever thought about why you're here and what your purpose is? It's something we all wonder about sometimes. Finding meaning and purpose gives me a sense of direction and happiness like a guiding light showing the way. Discovering your mission is like discovering your soul, what your passions are, what makes you feel excited, and what fuels you. Your soul guides you to your calling.

Understanding your aim in life is about what makes you truly happy in what you do. Everyone has a purpose in life. For some it is being in service of others, as they feel happy when they can help others, People with such a mission go into professions where they can serve others, such as social work or law enforcement, or they work in nonprofit organizations for humanitarian causes. They could do anything they feel that drives their passion. Some could be authors who write to inspire and motivate others.

I am fortunate to have many interests and passions, and I do not have time to be bored, as they keep me occupied. These passions are like an engine that keeps me going. Whether it's painting or helping others, embracing my passions can give me a deeper sense of direction. When I do things that I love, it opens doors to a more fulfilling life. There is a relevant saying: "When you love what you do, it will never feel like work."

You, too, can dive deep into the depths of your soul and see what is it that motivates you. What makes you happy? What do you do that brings you joy? What can you spend time doing without realizing that time is flying by? Your aim in life does not have to be the same as your parents' family members', or even friends'; you are your unique self. You have your role and your purpose; follow the path you are meant to be on.

My main passion in life is helping people in any way I can, and next to that is my passion for arts and crafts. These two things that I am passionate about bring me great joy, and I feel fortunate to know what I have interests in. I have friends who have been so busy with life and working and earning a living but do not have any idea what their interests are. They have careers but no hobbies, and when they are nearing retirement age, they dread the thought of not knowing what to do with their lives after they retire.

I highly recommend that if you still have a ways to go before you retire from your job and do not know what your interests are, you take a journey inside of you to become more aware of yourself and to learn what brings you joy or what triggers you. It is time to get to know yourself better so you do not suddenly feel lost.

Values are like personal guidebook for life choices. They tell you what's important and shape how you want to live. You look at the qualities you admire in others and aim to reflect them in yourself. Honesty, kindness, creativity—are these things you value? When you live by your values, life feels more meaningful. Let your values be like a compass that points you to actions that feel right for you.

Life is all about growing and learning, and all of my experiences, even the tough ones, help me become better. Challenges, especially, give me chances to learn and become stronger. You can welcome challenges as steps that help you reach a purposeful life. When you look at tough times with a positive attitude, you can change them into things that make you grow and become a better person.

When you go through your challenges, allow yourself to accept them in order for you to grow. Learn to become stronger and more resilient, which helps you to deal with any challenge that you may encounter in the future. Resisting prevents you from growing and also prevents you from achieving happiness in life.

Having good connections with others is a big part of finding meaning and purpose. Building and keeping special relationships makes us feel as though we belong and have friends. I reach out to people who make me feel good and share my goals. These connections create a group of people who encourage me to follow my passions and purpose. Together, we can create a web of shared experiences that make our lives special. I am very fortunate to have a very supportive circle around me.

At the centre of finding meaning and purpose is wanting to help something beyond just us. This could mean making good changes in our community, in nature, and in the lives of others. Doing nice things, volunteering, or working for a bigger cause can make me feel as though I have a purpose that's more than just about me. I volunteer at Hospice Georgina, Good Food Collective, and Routes Connecting Community. It brings me great joy to know that I'm making a positive impact in the lives of people I come into contact with. I realize small changes can be made in the world in my way.

Have you ever been so into something that you didn't even notice time passing? That's called "flow," and it feels amazing. When you are in the flow, you are totally focused on what you are doing. These are the moments when you often find the most meaning and purpose, whether you are solving a puzzle, listening to music, or making something creative. I can do things that let me experience the flow feeling. These moments show me how much I can enjoy a life that has a purpose. I often am in the flow during creative moments.

Being thankful is a powerful tool that can help us find more meaning and purpose. Every day, we can take a moment to think about what we are grateful for—big or small. When we are thankful, we can change our focus from what we don't have to what we do have. This makes us look at life in a positive way. When we appreciate the good things around us, we start to see how rich and meaningful my everyday life is. Gratitude helps us see the beauty in life and makes our connection to its meaning strong.

Finding meaning and direction in life is a journey that takes time and thought. It's about knowing our passions, living by our values, growing as people, having important relationships, helping others, finding flow moments, and being grateful. Having an attitude of gratitude also helps us to see things in a positive light. Finding purpose involves diving deep within your inner self to find what makes you happy and what makes your heart and soul sing, and that brings you meaning and happiness.

## 3. Embracing Growth

In life, I've learned that the pursuit of perfection isn't the real goal. It's more about embracing imperfections, which leads to genuine personal growth and fulfilment. This realization has been a game-changer for me; it's helped me overcome challenges, nurture self-compassion, and explore new possibilities. Embracing imperfections has given me a sense of freedom and joy that I'd love to share with others.

When I mention imperfections, I'm talking about those little quirks and mistakes that make us beautifully human. I used to feel an immense pressure to be flawless—to have all the answers and never make a mistake. But I've come to understand that this mindset leads only to stress and frustration. None of us are perfect, and that's perfectly fine.

Accepting my imperfections felt like dropping a heavy weight, finally allowing myself to breathe. Through my life experiences, especially during challenging health moments, I've learned to be kind to myself and accept my flaws. I had no choice, as otherwise I would have made myself sicker.

Accepting imperfection isn't about settling for less; it's about recognizing that our flaws are part of what makes us unique. Once I started seeing my imperfections as part of who I am, I began appreciating myself more.

One of the most important lessons I've learned is that imperfection doesn't mean I am a failure. Mistakes aren't setbacks; they're lessons waiting to be learned. Instead of mistakes, I see them as stepping stones guiding me towards a better version of myself.

The Healing Journey Program focuses on embracing yourself, including those traits you might see as flaws. When you commit to this programme, you start by listing what you like and dislike about yourself. Then you are guided to accept the things you dislike by highlighting the strengths that come with them, helping you embrace them as part of who you are. This isn't about physical attributes; it's about you as a person. Once you realize the powerful gifts within your dislike list, you learn to appreciate the uniqueness that makes you special.

Embracing growth goes hand in hand with accepting imperfection. It's about being open to change, new experiences, and becoming the best version of yourself. Growth isn't a linear path; it's full of twists and turns. Sometimes you stumble, but that doesn't mean you are lost. It means you are learning and evolving.

Growth often involves stepping out of our comfort zones. Staying in the safe zone is easy, but the real magic happens beyond it. We may discover that trying new things, even though a bit scary, can lead to amazing opportunities. Each time you take that leap, you surprise yourself with what you can achieve. I encourage you to conquer those fears holding you back, take risks, and embrace the magic of new experiences.

It's crucial that we surround ourselves with positivity and support on this journey. Connecting with like-minded individuals who share similar goals can be incredibly empowering. Together we lift each other, celebrate victories, and lend a helping hand. Building community fuels growth and celebrates imperfections.

Practising self-compassion has been a game-changer for me. Just as I'd comfort a friend facing a challenge, I've learned to extend that kindness to myself. This self-love fuels my motivation and helps me bounce back from setbacks. It wasn't easy at first, but I had to learn to be my own supporter.

Setting goals is an essential part of embracing growth—not unrealistic goals, but goals that push you a little further. They give you direction and a sense of purpose. With every milestone achieved, you feel a sense of accomplishment that pushes you to aim higher. Starting with small, achievable goals can be a great way to build motivation to reach for bigger ones.

It has been fulfilling for me to watch a student of mine learn not to overwhelm herself by thinking how big the task is and end up preventing herself from getting started, but rather to be kind to herself and tell herself she will do a small, achievable amount. Once that is achieved, she has the option to stop and be happy she got started, or she can continue and do a bit more because now she feels motivated to continue. Just this simple change in getting started has helped her to tackle all her other tasks that she once used to procrastinate on.

This change has started a new habit of not only being kind to herself but also achieving tasks that used to feel too daunting to start. Accepting imperfection and embracing growth have become my guiding principles. They've transformed how people approach challenges and opportunities. Embracing imperfections has given people the freedom to be themselves and has opened doors to growth that they never imagined possible.

This journey demands patience, self-compassion, and a willingness to face the unknown, even if it's daunting. But the rewards—the sense of achievement and the joy of becoming the best version of oneself—make every step worthwhile. I invite you to join me on this journey of embracing imperfection and experiencing the transformative power of growth.

## 4. Self-Reflection and Inner Awareness

You will learn that taking a moment to look within yourself can lead to wonderful discoveries. It's like having a conversation with your own heart and mind. I did this a lot when I left my arranged marriage. This process is called self-reflection, and it's a way of understanding who I am and how I feel. I strongly believe in self-awareness and will continue to stress the importance of self-awareness throughout this book, as it is the key to finding ourselves and knowing what it is in life that we value and want for ourselves.

Self-reflection is like looking in a mirror, but instead of seeing my physical appearance, I'm delving into my thoughts, emotions, and experiences. It's a chance to stop and ask myself questions like "How am I feeling today?" or "What did I learn from that experience?" This simple act of asking myself questions opens a door to understanding my inner world.

One way I practise self-reflection is through journaling. Take a few minutes each day or each week, depending on how much time you have in a day, to write down your thoughts and feelings. It's like having a private conversation with yourself on paper. You can look back at your journal and see how you've grown and changed over time. To those of you who enjoy journaling digitally (this is more the younger generations, who find it easier than recording things with pen and paper), this is fine as well, as long as you are taking notes on your daily or weekly events.

The Healing Journey Program is like having a personal journal where you jot down your thoughts about your day, how you handled the challenges that popped up, and how you interacted with the people you met. We go through these things together, and I help you see more about yourself through these notes in your journal.

Gaining inner awareness is like learning more about your inner thoughts and feelings. It's about being curious about your mind. When you pay attention to your thoughts, you start noticing some regular patterns. For instance, you might realize you often worry about what's coming up next or that certain things light up your day. Noticing these patterns helps you jot them down and think about changes you would like to make.

Knowing how you feel is important too. Emotions are like little messages from your heart telling you how you're taking in different situations. When you tune in to these feelings, you can respond in a much healthier way. Feeling stressed? It might be time to take a breather, go for a walk, or even just listen to some relaxing tunes. For me, after a workshop, I love diving into some crafts to unwind. Finding what makes you happy can help relieve stress too.

Self-reflection and inner awareness are like tools to help you through life. They help you make smarter choices and understand yourself on a deeper level. When you get used to reflecting and being aware, you start recognizing what you need and want in life. Some people find meditation super helpful. But for me, my kind of meditation is more active—I do something that doesn't require too much thinking, such as taking a stroll or doing repetitive tasks that give my brain a break. You don't have to do the "sit in a special position and be super quiet" kind of meditation. Find your way to calm that mind down!

These practices have various advantages. They're key to helping you manage stress and tough feelings. Knowing why you feel a certain way can help you cope better. Feeling overloaded? A break spent doing what you enjoy can do wonders to lift your spirits. That is what I do for myself.

They also do wonders for your relationships. When you're clued into your thoughts and feelings, you can talk better with those around you. For example, if something's bothering you, you can talk about how you feel and why. It opens doors for heart-to-heart conversations and closer connections.

And let's not forget self-reflection and inner awareness. They're like confidence boosters. Pat yourself on the back when you spot your strengths and achieve those goals. In a world that's super busy and loud, taking time for yourself is like giving yourself a present. It's a chance to slow down, hang out with yourself, and find some clarity. It's a way to take care of your well-being.

When clients achieve their goals or items on their wish lists (lists I get them to write about what they hope to accomplish from the Healing Journey Program), I encourage them to recognize and acknowledge their success in achieving their goals and award themselves with gold stars or even treat themselves to something special they feel they deserve.

# 5. Your Unique Journey

Everyone experiences life differently; therefore, each person's destination in life is different, meaning a person's journey is unique to him or her. You are on your own journey, so it's best never to compare your life to those around you, because you are different from those around you. The way you think, feel, and act will be different according to your interests and values; therefore, your journey cannot be compared with the journeys of others.

Each person's journey is guided by his or her own set of values and principles he or she lives by. Everyone has a set of dreams or goals he or she hopes to achieve. You write your own story based on where you are and where you want to be going forward. If you feel you are not happy with a certain outcome, then you will want to change the outcome by doing things differently based on the lessons you have learned from your experiences.

If you are not sure how to go about making the changes and feel stuck in an unhappy state, this is where I step in to help guide you to learn more about yourself and to realize what it is you need to achieve what you want to achieve to make you happy.

The journey is not always easy if you are willing to be committed to your growth and put in the effort to learn from experiences and open your mind to see where you have set yourself up for any issues you are dealing with. You learn to have a clearer picture of the restrictions you have placed upon yourself in moving forward from your situations, whether they be based in fear or unawareness.

Life is like a puzzle made up of all the things you do, the choices you make, the good times, and the rough times. Each moment contributes to your story and shapes who you are. It is important to first be okay with who you are and then identify aspects of yourself that you do not like and can improve upon.

When you recognize and work on these areas, it's essential to celebrate your growth and transformation. Think of it as giving yourself a big hug and rewarding yourself for your willingness to learn, grow, and move forward. Being content with who you are means you won't worry about whether others like you, because you already do and you don't need anyone's approval to be the person you are.

If you find yourself comparing yourself to others, remind yourself that you are not them and they are not you. When you see others on social media and feel inadequate when comparing yourself to them, remember that what you see on social media is not always accurate. That is why it is best to see yourself from within and know you are worthy as you are. If you feel you are not worthy, ask yourself why. If there is something you can do to improve yourself, then do so. You want to grow according to your inner values, not what you see others doing.

Some amazing people in history celebrated their special journeys too. They didn't do things the usual way, but they changed the world. People like Steve Jobs, Oprah Winfrey, and Malala Yousafzai had challenges, but they didn't give up. They believed in themselves and what they were doing. Their stories show that when you're proud of who you are and what you're doing, you can make a big difference.

Life is not always easy or a straight line. It has its ups and downs. By acknowledging that you can get through this, over time you will learn not to let your challenges throw you down but will instead catch yourself from falling too far down and pick yourself up. You will learn to get through life's challenges with fewer extreme lows because you learn to recover your balance sooner after you experience lows.

Celebrating your journey does not mean you must ignore other people's journeys, because everyone in your life brings in something unique to your journey as well. When you are proud of yourself, you also learn to appreciate others and respect them as well.

This helps to make the world a nicer place where everyone

is important. When you know your story matters, you also learn that other people's stories are important as well. This realization helps you to form better connections with others and brings you closer, even though they may be different from you. It is like a big family where everyone cares for each other.

You don't need others to tell you that you're great; you feel it inside. When you're happy about what you've done, you spread good feelings to others too. Don't forget the people who have helped you on your journey. Family, friends, teachers—they're all part of your story. Saying "thank you" to them is like giving them a warm hug. It shows you appreciate what they've done for you. Being grateful is the most important part of the journey. Having a grateful heart helps you to see things in a positive light.

## 6. Self-Discovery with Present Awareness

Life is never stagnant; it is full of surprises, which I am sure you already know by now through your own experiences. As we journey through life, we learn more about ourselves and the world around us if we are paying close attention to everything around us or with us.

When you choose to be aware of your every moment, you will be surprised how much you can learn from each moment that passes. I know I am, because I keep myself open to take note when opportunity comes knocking for me to learn helpful new information or new skills.

Being present in the moment helps us be aware of everything around us. We learn about ourselves when we observe how we react to circumstances and situations that we go through.

Similarly, if you are strolling along in a garden filled with flowers and you allow yourself to take in everything in the garden, observing what types of flowers are there in front of you, you will be able to enjoy not only the beauty of the flowers in front of you but also the lovely fragrances these flowers emit.

If you are not present in the moment while you stroll along the garden and your mind is off somewhere in the future or the past, you may not be able to be present to what is in front of you and enjoy what nature has to offer. In the same way, when you are present in the moment, there are many subtle changes that occur within, and you will be able to experience those changes and transformations.

When I cook, I do not follow any specific recipe. I allow my instincts to help me put together ingredients at my disposal. By nature, I am not a follower, and I am not good at following anyone's recipe; I usually create my own. I follow my inner guidance.

We can learn how to deal with our life situations by being creative in how we solve our problems, instead of worrying about not having the recipe to solve the issue we are dealing with. Be creative and whip up your own recipe to solve whatever problems may arise. We can do this when we are present in the moment so we are able to see what is in front of us.

It is okay to daydream from time to time to escape from the heavy reality, but we must also be aware of what is around us so we do not miss what may pass by us when we are not paying attention. It's as though we are drifting on a boat, passing by beautiful scenery.

You may want to look around you and take in the beauty that is passing you by as you float past and truly take in the beauty and wonder around you instead of floating on the boat with your eyes closed. If you have your eyes closed, you will not be able to see what you have missed and what has passed you by.

Life is very much like that; it comes and passes you by. By paying attention and being aware, you are able to benefit from what you see in front of you as it passes you by. I registered for all the programmes that are offered at YSpace–Georgina.

I keep myself open to all the programmes to help small businesses to succeed. I am at a stage in my life where I am making changes and going in a new direction from being a full-time florist and part-time holistic healer to being a full-time holistic healer and part-time florist.

By being open to taking advantage of programs offered by the Town of Georgina through YSpace, I am learning new skills to help my business grow, including technology skills once thought unattainable. This openness helps with personal growth and awareness that we can achieve our goals if we work towards them. I did not allow fear to prevent me from learning new skills and adapting.

I have become aware that I do, in fact, enjoy being creative using technology. We just never know what we can learn about ourselves. A year ago, I would never have imagined that I would love what I do nowadays. That is why it is so important that we do not allow fear to stop us from learning and growing.

Overcoming fear is one of the key skills taught to my clients so they can learn to become self-aware and let go of what does not serve them. It is okay to charge ahead despite any fears and see what you can achieve. Being present is like allowing yourself to feel the warmth of the sun upon your face or being aware of where you are going or where you are at the moment.

Have you ever blown bubbles and watched them float away? Each bubble is unique, just like you. As you watch them glide through the air, you're focused on their beauty. You are the only person who can create your own reality by following your own path of self-discovery. Enjoy each moment as you go through it, be proud of your progress, and be happy where you have reached. This self-awareness is what will enrich your life and your purpose.

# Chapter 8

*Trusting the Timing of Life*

## 1. Patience and Trust

LIFE IS A JOURNEY, AND LIKE ANY JOURNEY, IT HOLDS UNEXPECTED surprises. When you are travelling by air, you may encounter flights being delayed or cancelled, or there may be an unexpected change of boarding gate because the airline decides to change planes. Or, if you are travelling by car, you may encounter traffic jams due to an accident ahead. No matter how well you plan your trip, you can never predict how it will go with certainty, as there is always the possibility of unpredictable events.

No matter how well we may have planned our lives or what we like to do or where we want to be in our futures, there is always a possibility that unexpected events may change our plans, just as we may have to change course when we go on a journey. The plane may have to take a detour because of weather conditions or any unexpected issues that may arise.

We must therefore always be prepared for any surprise and have patience and allow the process to take us on a detour. Some of these unexpected events may arise to teach us a lesson that we may need to help us in the future. Sometimes they could also take us on a beautiful scenic route that we would never have witnessed had the unexpected events not occurred.

Challenges and setbacks are not roadblocks; they are opportunities for growth. When you encounter obstacles, it's natural to feel frustrated or anxious. If you maintain patience and remain calm, you can navigate through the challenges that you encounter. Having patience has been my strength and has helped me through many difficult situations.

When I used to work in a flower shop, during the floral holiday season, we would have work overload, and everyone around me would be anxious and stressed about the amount of work at hand whether we could get through the work and meet the delivery deadlines.

I would somehow find myself going into a very calm state, and patience would set in, and I would find myself able to breeze through the work with no issue. Looking back, I think I always trusted the inner guidance I received to have patience, remain calm, and trust the process.

Having trust in the process and maintaining patience helps us through many obstacles because it helps us to view situations with a clearer perception. After all, when we are anxious or nervous, it is difficult to have an objective view of the situation at hand. We must try to learn to trust that everything happens in divine timing. Sometimes it may not be easy to see something, or things may seem off and not go well, and the outcome will not be what we hope for.

If we allow ourselves to learn to trust in divine timing, we will soon learn that things do happen for the better even if it may not seem so. With patience, we soon learn that even though things may not go as we hoped, ultimately the outcome will be much better than what we hoped for.

Similarly, the process of trusting life's timing involves nurturing your dreams and goals. Just as you water a plant and give it sunlight, you must invest effort into your aspirations. But remember, growth takes time. A tree doesn't worry about when it will bear fruit; it simply grows and evolves naturally. By observing nature, you can understand the beauty of patience and the magic of timing.

Trusting the timing of your life means that looking back and looking for the pattern and recognizing that the steps you have taken have led you to where you are today. Every minute step plays a significant role in getting you to where you are. Sometimes subtle events can cause a significant impact and change.

I am glad that I am grateful for all of the experiences life threw at me. No matter how painful they were, I accepted them gracefully and trusted that there was a purpose for everything. To truly trust this timing, you must be flexible and be ready and open to what shows up. Being impatient and rigid can lead to resistance, while flexibility allows you to go with the flow.

Flexibility doesn't mean giving up on your goals; it means being open to different options that are available to you that might lead you to the same destination. I feel that when we resist our growth, we lose the lesson we could learn to have a more fulfilling life. I am grateful that I have seldom been resistant to what life has offered me. I gracefully accept all challenges because I know nothing stays the same and that problems will not remain forever. I often tell myself, "This, too, shall pass."

Always remember to acknowledge and celebrate your accomplishments no matter how small they are. Trust involves acknowledging your achievements. Every step you take forward in achieving your goals is a testament to your patience and your faith in the process, which fuels your trust and patience in your journey ahead. And remember: this is not a one-time process. It's a mindset you build over time. Some days it will be easy, while other days your logic may interfere and put doubts into your head. That is when you will need to allow yourself to trust in the guidance you receive within; that is where true magic lies.

## 2. Divine Timing

We all know that life is full of surprises and very complex. But people are just as complex and full of surprises. I am sure you have observed and experienced this first-hand. When dealing with people, we never know what to expect. Divine timing means perfect timing. Just like people and life, divine timing, too, is full of surprises.

The beauty of divine timing is that it flows and goes at its own pace. The most surprising thing is that things happen when we least expect them. Perfect timing is a surprise story that is fun and exciting. As an artist, you may start with a blank canvas and a selection of paints of different colours and you have a rough idea of what you want to paint or create, but along the way, you get an inspiration that surprises you, and you decide to paint what comes to you and are pleasantly surprised. You find that you finally created something you have always wanted, but somehow the inspiration didn't come through. But then—*boom!* Suddenly it comes through, and you were able to do so. I call that divine timing. You can create at the perfect time when such creations need to be created and shown.

You paint your picture using the colours you have at your disposal, and you can paint the picture as you are inspired to. Sometimes you feel so inspired that you create a beautiful work of art. When creativity flows beautifully, that is divine timing. I have found that when I am not well, I can create a beautiful work of art that lifts my spirits, and I then feel better.

Climbing a big hill is like going on an adventure. It takes time and effort, but when you get to the top, the view is amazing! Life is a bit like this too. It has ups and downs, and sometimes the best moments happen after a bit of waiting. These moments are like reaching the top of the hill and feeling so proud of what you did. When you look down, you see how far up you have climbed and say to yourself, "Wow! I did it."

I had an amazing spiritual experience when I was at the lowest moment of my life shortly after leaving my marriage and losing my father to cancer simultaneously. I also had a breast lumpectomy the same week as my father's burial. I felt I lost all my strength while dealing with all these events in my life.

I lay down in bed feeling hopeless and prayed for some help, and soon after I had a vision. I was clinging to the top of a mountain, hanging on but too tired to climb further up. I then felt I was directed to look down and see how far up I had climbed, and that I should not give up but should take a break to recover some strength, as the top was within reach. I consider that divine timing in helping me out of a feelings of despair.

Meeting new friends can feel like a big adventure. Sometimes you meet someone at just the right time, and it feels like magic. This is perfect timing at work. The world sets things up so you can meet people who become important in your life. It's like making new characters in your story. I can say this has been true for me in many instances. I meet the right people when I need assistance in certain circumstances in my life.

If you think back in time, you may be able to confirm to yourself that meeting the right people at the right time is something you, too, have experienced. When you think about your life, you can find moments that changed everything. These moments might not have made sense at first, but looking back, you can see how they fit together. These special times are like puzzle pieces of perfect timing. They make your life story wonderful.

## 3. Letting Go of Control

It is common and very natural for people to want to have some control over some things in life, while there are also people who go overboard and want to have control over everything and everyone. Some people like to have control because they feel they will be able to manage things just the way they want to be. When things do not go their way, they are angry and upset and get out of control themselves.

Individuals who have experienced childhood trauma may feel insecure or have insecurities or lack self-confidence because they had no control over the situations they experienced. They subconsciously often want to have control over everything when they are adults because they feel that as adults on their own, parents and elders are no longer in control of their lives as they were when they were younger.

Imagine that you have a big balloon and you are holding it tight so it won't fly away, you think that you are in control and that as long as you hold it tight it won't fly away. However, a strong wind could carry your balloon away no matter how tightly you hold it. In the same way, life can be very much like that. You may think you have control over things, and you may want things to go just as you want them to. You may think you can decide how your day should be or what others should do. But life is like the wind, constantly changing. No matter how much you want and expect things to go the way you want them to, life brings unexpected changes and challenges.

Some neat freaks and those who have obsessive-compulsive disorder (OCD) may have had tough times growing up and were unable to control what was happening with them. They started to keep things super tidy because that was something they could control. I went through something similar. I kept my own surroundings super neat and tidy and even decorated my own space.

However, I began going through unexpected health challenges that made it impossible for me to keep things as neat and tidy as I was used to because my body did not cooperate with my mind. It became a stressor for me because I was lying in bed suffering from excruciating and debilitating pain. I had to accept the circumstances I was in and had to learn to let go of the fact that I must be able to clean my home constantly and keep it as neat as I wanted.

It was upsetting for me that I couldn't do anything. I had to learn to adapt. I had to let go of the need to want to have my house neat and tidy. I had no control of it. I had to learn to be okay because life can surprise us. As we go through life, things happen, and there is nothing we can do to have control over things we want.

When we stop trying to control everything, we open ourselves up to life's natural flow. By not stressing over things we can't change, we find peace even when things do not go as we planned. It's about realizing that true control comes from how we react to unpredictable situations, not from trying to control everything. Accepting the unpredictable and handling things as they come is often the best approach.

After all, we can't always foresee what's ahead. I describe a friend of mine as "predictably unpredictable." Nothing this person does surprises me, and I am okay with that and am not upset by it, as there are no expectations.

## 4. Surrendering to Life's flow

While helping others heal, a frequent theme arises in stories of how people desire control. They often express a need to manage not only their actions and behaviours but also those of others. This often leads to having certain expectations, and when these expectations aren't met, they feel a sense of loss of control, which in turn leads to feelings of disappointment and further loss of control.

Such circumstances lead to anger and resentment, which in turn lead to conflicts, and vicious cycles begin. Feelings of frustration and anger become the root cause of conflicts that strain relationships. The goal is to assist clients in releasing the need for excessive control. I work with them gradually to build trust and encourage surrendering the need for control. By embracing a more flexible approach and learning to go with the flow, they can experience a liberating sense of freedom. This process involves letting go of unrealistic expectations of both themselves and others.

It may seem or feel as if it is a sign of weakness if you allow yourself to let go and go with the flow, because you may think that you are yielding or waving a white flag in the face of challenges. But in reality, it takes courage to recognize that sometimes there are forces that are beyond our control, and then when we resist, it can be exhausting and frustrating.

Yielding is a conscious decision to let go of personal expectations and desires and learning to trust that the universe has its own purpose and knows best, and letting go is allowing the universe to take the lead and show us what is good for us, as every situation has its own lessons and purpose.

When you allow yourself to trust in the universe, you no longer carry a heavy weight that is weighing you down. You open yourself up to the changes and adjust yourself to the changes as they show up. You begin to feel the sense of calm by allowing life to unfold itself. As you go through these changes, letting go of control brings you a unique kind of tranquillity.

When clients begin to let go of their need for control, there is a shift in their perspectives towards life. Their way of perceiving and interpreting things transforms. They become less defensive and more receptive to being more cordial and understanding. They also become more approachable, as observed by others, and easier to talk to.

When things get tough, surrendering is like finding a safe spot in the middle of a storm. It's a way to take a break from struggling and find peace even when everything seems chaotic. It doesn't mean giving up completely. We need to conserve our energy and not waste it on menial things that cause us stress. Instead it means focusing our energy on finding a way through and following the wisdom of life. That is why I prefer not to react to the stressors around me and remain calm. This is how I conserve my energy.

Finding peace in surrendering to life's flow is a continuous practice, a journey of trust and surrender. It's not always easy, and there will be moments when we want to take control again. Yet, in those moments, we remind ourselves of the serenity that comes from allowing life to lead. And in this surrender, we find a meaningful and lasting peace that goes beyond the ups and downs of life's journey.

## 5. Embracing Synchronicity

You may have heard the phrase "There are no coincidences." The term "synchronicity" refers to meaningful coincidences. Things happen for a reason or we meet people for a reason. Allowing synchronicity in relationships involves acknowledging that every person who enters our lives does so with a purpose. I believe this to be true for myself because I am aware of how each person has impacted my life.

People we meet mirror our strengths, challenge our limitations, or teach us lessons. You may have heard the phrase, "People enter our lives for a reason, season, or lifetime." If you examine the people in your life—how you met them and what and how they have contributed to your life—you will be able to understand what I mean about meeting a person being no coincidence.

If you are open to personal and spiritual growth, you may understand that each person that enters our lives has a lesson to teach us. Some difficult people teach us patience, and abusers teach us or bring out our inner strength. We are constantly learning to grow and improve through the relationships we encounter in our daily lives. It is up to us to either grow from the experiences to become better people or not.

I examine how life experiences shape us into who we are. I've personally chosen to grow from these experiences, believing we all have the power to make that choice. You, too, have the power to choose how you let your life experiences shape you. You are truly in charge of your own life.

Recognizing the connections we share with others leads us on a journey of self-discovery. Every interaction, no matter how brief, leaves a mark on us. Trusting the universe's flow has enriched my journey, bringing the right people and opportunities at just the right moments. Sometimes we can meet someone on the street for a brief moment, and that person may say something—something brief, or even a word—that leaves a lasting impression.

Intuition, our inner guide, helps us navigate synchronicity—the meaningful coincidences that shape our path. Cultivating trust in our intuition allows us to notice signs leading us forward, even if they defy logic. When you trust in your intuition, you will know how beneficial it is to listen to that inner voice.

When facilitating Tap into Your Intuition workshops, the emphasis is on intuition's power. It is crucial in guiding us towards our purpose. Synchronicity, unlike typical cause-and-effect science, reveals the deeper connections in our world. We often feel a strong connection with others without knowing why, only later seeing their roles in our lives. Some people may think they are not intuitive, but if they practise going within and try to listen to the subtle inner voice, they, too, can develop their intuition.

These seemingly insignificant moments hold immense power. Over time, their purpose becomes clear, guiding us to brighter destinations. Embracing synchronicity helps us navigate life's challenges with greater ease. To accept synchronicity, we need to shift our perspective, accepting and opening our door to allow the unknown to enter with curiosity. This promotes personal and spiritual growth, which changes our perception of the world and develops a more positive outlook.

Symbols, such as repeated numbers and signs in dreams, hold meaning. Decoding these symbols helps us understand the unfolding of events. You may have seen repeated numbers while driving, such as a car's licence plate containing 333, 777, or 444, or noticed a clock reading 5:55 or 11:11. These numbers all have meanings. There is plenty of information available online about the significance of such numbers (https://www.allure.com/story/ what-are-angel-numbers). When you see these numbers, consider examining what's happening in your life and how the meaning of the number makes sense. If not, watch for what might transpire next.

Synchronicity invites us to enjoy life's mysteries and trust the signs from the universe. It's a path of discovery that leads to a richer life

## 6. Heart's Timing in Relationships and Career

Earlier on I talked about divine timing. There are times when we all feel that we are at a crossroads and we need to make a decision on which path to take. In situations like these, we all feel torn about which path is the right one. If you choose one and regret it, you may think, "Oh, I should have gone the other way." It is very natural for us to doubt ourselves sometimes.

No matter what the decision may relate to—whether it be a matter of the heart, a career, or certain goals you have set for yourself—it is so easy to get caught up in the rush, wanting instant gratification. Sadly, things do not materialize when we want them to happen. The best things you can do for yourself are have patience, allow divine timing to take its course, and trust your heart. Step back and trust the timing of your heart. Your heart will let you know when the time is right to make any life-altering decisions.

Matters of the heart can be unique and complicated. You may have heard the phrases "We do not choose who we fall in love with" and "The heart wants what the heart wants or who the heart wants." Love is a journey all on its own, and here I am talking about romantic love. Sometimes you meet someone and you feel an instant connection, and sometimes it takes a while for the spark to ignite.

It is important to remember that there is no set timeline for falling in love. I am sure you have time and time again heard friends, colleagues, or even acquaintances talk about how they met their partners, how they weren't expecting it, and how it just happened, and so on and so forth. You never know when the cupid will hit you or even whether it will.

Some people are very fortunate to be able to fall in love with a person who is a perfect match for them, and their love thrives and sees them through difficult times. In such cases, I would safely assume that the couple has been open to growing together, learning to adapt and compromise, and creating a safe space for themselves to be their authentic selves by being open, honest, and willing to share and communicate without reservation.

Trust in any relationship is important, whether it be a romantic one or between family and friends. When you allow love to unfold naturally, it tends to be genuine and enduring. Trust your instincts and let the connection evolve at its own pace. Everyone has a path of his or her own, and each has a unique path because different people have different skills and aspirations.

Relationships need time and nurturing to grow. Rushing into something or trying to force feelings can lead to misunderstandings or heartache. This is often true in instances when people rely on physical attraction and ignore all the warning signs on how another person may not be a good match. As the saying goes, the heart wants what or who the heart wants, irrespective of whether it is good or not.

Now let's shift our focus to the world of work. Careers are like a puzzle; each piece fits in its own time. You might see others speeding ahead, achieving milestones that you wish to reach. But remember: their path is not your own. Your career journey is unique, based on your skills, experiences, and opportunities.

Trust that your path is leading you exactly where you need to be. I know it has been so for myself.

I set out to do holistic healing offering reiki and reflexology. as time progressed, my holistic practice evolved from servicing clients to helping relieve chronic pain. But it evolved into servicing and helping others in mental well-being as I allowed my guidance to lead me to where I should go. When I decided to be a holistic practitioner with the hope of helping others with their physical pain, it did not remotely occur to me that it would take me in the direction of helping their mental and emotional well-being.

My interests have been in arts and crafts, and I spent most of my formative years indulging in arts and crafts, specifically making flowers in my early teens. I never imagined back then that someday I would be a floral designer, but I have been one for almost four decades. Currently I am even considering incorporating my artistic skills into my healing practice in the form of art therapy. The possibilities are endless when we allow ourselves to just go with the flow and let life unfold what the universe has in store for us.

Sometimes setbacks or delays in your career can be blessings in disguise. My setback was my health challenges while I worked as a floral designer. Because of that, I sought alternative healing, which led me to reiki and reflexology, which led me to my current profession. Setbacks can provide you with chances to learn, grow, and refine your skills. It's like baking a cake—you can't rush the process; each ingredient needs its time to blend and rise. For me, it led me to adopt a new path as a holistic practitioner.

People often change careers at least twice in their lifetimes. (https://study.uq.edu.au/stories/how-many-career-changes-lifetime#:~:text=Research%20shows%20most%20people%20will,and%20upcoming%20generations%20of%20workers). Additionally, most people do not end up working in the profession they were originally trained or educated for.

Oftentimes, people choose a profession because it offers a

good salary, but it may not be what the heart desires, and sadly, these people end up unhappy in their jobs. No matter what happens in life, trust in the universe, your heart, and where your heart leads you. Your heart will lead to a job that you will enjoy doing.

Faith is key. It's about believing in yourself and the path you're on. Even when things seem uncertain, trust that each step is taking you somewhere important. My strong faith has been my anchor through life's ups and downs. It's what gave me strength and guided me forward. I held on to the belief that everything would fall into place as long as I accepted the challenges and let them shape me.

Trusting your heart's timing is a powerful practice in both relationships and careers. It's about acknowledging that life has its own pace, and that's perfectly okay. Continue on your journey and know that every step, whether fast or slow, is part of your unique story.

As you go through the complexities of love and work, remember to be kind to yourself. Trust your heart, and have faith that you are exactly where you need to be right now. The best chapters of your life are often written in the perfect timing of your heart. Trust in the divine timing, and have faith and patience.

# Chapter 9

## Empathy and Compassion

## 1. Power of Empathy

THE CONCEPTS OF EMPATHY AND SYMPATHY ARE VERY SIMILAR, but there is a distinctive difference between the two. Sympathy is the ability to understand or feel pity for another person's misfortune, whereas being an empath myself, I can empathize with what others are experiencing. It is not a pity that I feel. I can literally feel what others are going through, be it emotionally or physically.

Empathy has a profound impact on connecting with hearts and minds. Its strong forces shape our interactions and relationships. It is the ability to understand and share the feelings of another person, to step into his or her shoes and to view the world through his or her eyes. It often helps in a world where people often argue and fight. Empathy shines bright like a hopeful light. It brings us together, helps us understand each other, and makes things better. It is not about merely acknowledging another person's feelings, but really about genuinely experiencing and understanding how others feel and trying to see things from their perspectives. This helps to create bridges between individuals.

In my quest to understand who I am, in my mid-twenties, when I left my arranged marriage, I embarked on a journey of self-discovery and understanding of my inner self and my experiences that I had. I became aware that I was unlike many people in my network. I often felt what others do not feel, having an inner knowing of events that would unfold in the future and dreams that often came true. I did not know that I was experiencing many of these experiences because I am an empath.

Being unaware of the fact I am an empath, I struggled with these gifts. Over time I learned more about it and learned to manage these gifts to get through life without being bombarded with everyone's energies and emotions. I learned to protect myself from being affected by the energies of those around me and soon empowered myself with the knowledge of how to manage all the energies that were affecting my daily life.

Currently, I am teaching and empowering other empaths to do the same. Through my research into empathy, I discovered that the brain activity of empaths differs from that of non-empaths. Specifically, empaths have higher mirror neuron receptivity. This research is ongoing and continually evolving.

Neuroscientific research has shed light on the impact of empathy on the brain. When we empathize, our brains activate regions associated with both emotions and understanding, forging deep connection with the experiences of others.

In personal relationships, empathy acts as a binding agent to help build strong bonds. It promotes intimacy, trust, and mutual respect. When we truly understand and validate the feelings of our loved ones, we create a safe space for them to be vulnerable. This, in turn, creates a sense of belonging and strengthens the bonds that hold us together.

When there are conflicts or disagreements, empathy helps to resolve them with compassion. When you can empathize, the chance of conflict is low. It is then more likely that you will agree to disagree because you have a better understanding of the other person. Though your point of view is different from the other person's, you won't be in conflict, because you understand and respect others' thoughts and opinions.

Empathy is the key to effective and inspirational guidance. Team leaders need to understand the struggles, aspirations, and fears of their team members to promote a positive and productive environment. This helps create greater employee satisfaction and willingness to be more proactive in a company's success.

Clients who are in managerial positions are guided on the importance of being flexible and accepting. They are encouraged to guide and teach their teams with kindness and support, appreciating everyone's unique contributions and understanding that they have their own unique ways of doing tasks, and that means they may be different. It's all about finding ways that work well for the company without talking down to anyone, so the team feels valued and motivated instead of criticized.

Empathy helps break through any barriers we create and shows that deep down we are all the same. When we understand that we all face hardships no matter where we are or who we are, it inspires us to take action and speak up for change and make the world a fairer place for everyone. You likely have heard about people lending a helping hand following natural disasters; that is empathy in action.

For some of us, empathy is natural, but it is also something that one can learn and get better at, especially if one is around empathic people. Empathic people can inspire others through their acts of compassion and kindness. It is about opening our hearts and being ready to step into someone else's shoes. Understanding how others feel is very powerful, and it shifts our perspective on ourselves and helps us to get along better with others. It reminds us that no matter where we are from, we all experience similar emotions, which helps us to build connections and make the world a kinder and more compassionate place.

## 2. Connecting on a Deeper Level

I consider myself to be a deep person. Those who know me agree that is true of me. I have always been this way, as far back in my formative years. By nature, I tend to form deep connections with people I meet and get to know. In my circle of friends, we have deep connections.

The only people I may not have deep connections with are people that I like to keep a comfortable distance from—people that are too toxic or negative. I will still be polite and kind to them because that's who I am, but I will have healthy boundaries in such instances. I am willing to be of help if needed. I feel that deeper connections are meaningful and healthy. It's like building a strong bridge between hearts. This helps us understand each other better and creates lasting bonds. I have friends from pre-teens to classmates from college. Distance does not matter; we are there for each other when we need.

Connecting deeply with others is like planting a seed. When we take the time to truly listen and care, we nurture that seed into a strong, beautiful tree. This tree symbolizes a strong and lasting relationship. One of the most important things in connecting deeply is listening. This involves not just hearing words but also understanding feelings. When someone talks, listen carefully, and try to understand what the person means, not just what he or she says. This is important so you know how to offer support when needed.

Now let's talk about sharing. It's like giving a part of ourselves to others. When we open up about our thoughts and feelings, it creates a space for trust and understanding to grow. "Empathy" is a big word, but it simply means "understanding how someone else feels." It's like walking in someone else's shoes for a while. When we empathize, we show that we care about others' joys and sorrows. This strengthens our bond with them.

Patience is another important trait to have. Having patience is really rewarding in all areas of our lives. People always comment on me having lots of patience. I used to think I did not possess this trait, but I truly do in many areas of my life—however, maybe not in areas where people demonstrate ignorance. I do have patience when I am teaching.

Accepting each other's quirks, strengths, and even weaknesses is a key to deep connections. It's saying, "I accept you just the way you are. We're all like unique puzzle pieces. We can accept others if we know how to accept ourselves for who we are and are comfortable with our uniqueness. Accepting each other's quirks, strengths, and even weaknesses is a key to deep connections. It's saying, "I accept you just the way you are." Each one of us is unique in his or her own way, and we each have something to offer.

Similarly, in our relationships, we need to find common ground—things we and others enjoy or believe in. This strengthens our relationships and helps us grow together. Sometimes we get so busy with our thoughts that we forget to be present. When we're with someone, it's important to be there fully, in mind and heart. This shows that we value and respect the person's company, and it deepens our connection.

Although I have to admit I am guilty of multitasking at times, I am capable of absorbing and understanding what the other person is saying. There are times when I am multitasking and am having a conversation with someone on the phone, and if the conversation is sensitive, I will drop everything and be fully present.

In all types of relationships, there will be conflict at times. It's important to handle them with care and respect. Solving problems together strengthens the bond and helps us grow as individuals. Acknowledging each other's accomplishments shows that we are genuinely happy for each other's success, and it strengthens our bonds.

It is a precious gift if we can connect with others on a deeper level. We are giving ourselves to others and to people we care about. Remember: it's the small, heartfelt moments that make our connections strong and beautiful. So let's nurture our relationships and watch them grow into something truly special.

## 3. Practising Compassion for Self and Others

To show compassion to others, we must practise compassion for ourselves. To be compassionate to ourselves, we must first learn to accept and love ourselves. It is self-acceptance and self-love that breed love and acceptance of others most genuinely.

It is recommended that you start by listing everything you like or love about yourself, as well as everything you dislike. From that list, you are guided to learn how to accept and love the things you do not like about yourself, because quite often you may not realize that the very things that you do not like about yourself contain the key ingredient to help you to become more confident and even a better person.

Learning to accept ourselves and love ourselves helps us to understand when we need to set up healthy boundaries and have self-respect. In doing so, you learn also to respect others and their boundaries, which leads to having compassion for others. It helps you grow stronger and happier, and it spreads warmth and kindness to those around you.

Practising kindness for yourself and others is like growing a garden of love in your heart. It is common for people to feel a sense of abandonment or lack of love, especially by family members or life partners, which in turn affects their adult lives. When you start your healing journey, you learn to deal with these issues. Plant a tiny seed of love into your heart. As this seed grows, blooms, and produces more seeds, it spreads more and more love until it fills up all the empty spaces in the hearts of people that used to ache for love. This way you become good at loving yourself, and you don't need anyone else to make you feel

143

loved any more. This is basically what I have done for myself, and I teach others to do the same.

Learning to love oneself helps promote self-confidence and self-esteem, which is so vital in our daily interactions. Tell yourself, "I am perfectly imperfect, and that's what makes me special." No one is perfect, it's important to be okay with who you are. If you feel you have room for improvement, then learn to grow and improve yourself.

Learn to be gentle with yourself. Say, "You are doing the best you can, and that's enough." Acknowledge your achievements as well. Let go of your need to be perfect. You are perfect as you are with some room for improvement. You want to always have room for improvement, change, and growth.

Your body is a precious gift. Take care of it with love and attention. Say, "I will nourish myself with healthy food, rest, and exercise." Celebrate your victories, no matter how small. Acknowledge your efforts, and say, "I am proud of what I have accomplished."

Just as a fence protects a garden, boundaries protect your heart. Say, "It's okay to say no when I need to. My needs matter too."

When someone shares his or her thoughts or feelings, be present. Listen with your heart, not just your ears. Say, "I am here for you. You are important to me." Acts of kindness can be like a warm blanket on a cold day. Help when you can, and say, "How can I support you today?" Put yourself in the other person's shoes. Imagine how he or she feels. Say, "I understand, and I am here for you."

Holding on to grudges is like carrying a heavy stone. Forgive not because they deserve it but because you deserve peace. Say, "I release this burden, and I choose to move forward." Kindness is contagious. Be the spark that lights up someone's day. Say, "I choose to spread love and positivity wherever I go." Be the light and lead the way, or shine brightly to light up the path for others in their life's journey.

Having compassion for yourself and others is a lifelong journey. Remember: it's okay to take small steps. Each act of kindness, whether towards yourself or others, is like a drop in a pond, creating ripples that touch lives far beyond what you can see. So let your heart be a garden of compassion, and watch it bloom with beauty and warmth. Set an example for those around you.

## 4. Healing with Empathy

Love is a strong feeling that can make things better. I've heard many times that it can heal wounds. Maybe you've heard that too. In my life, I've seen love make things better. Does it fix everything? I'm not completely sure. What I do know is that if you let love into your heart, it can help heal the hurts inside. I'm talking about the emotional wounds, not the physical ones. However, even for physical hurts, if you treat them with lots of love and care, they can heal faster.

Healing wounds through understanding and empathy is a powerful way to make someone feel better, and it's something we can all do. Sometimes life can be tough. We all face difficulties and go through tough times. Empathetic understanding is like putting yourself in someone else's shoes. It means trying to feel what the other person is feeling, and understanding his or her pain or struggles.

Imagine that you are feeling sad or hurt. Wouldn't it be nice if someone tried to understand why you feel that way? When someone takes the time to understand how you're feeling, it can be like a warm hug for your heart. It makes you feel as though someone cares for you and as if you are not alone in your pain. We all want to feel as though someone understands and cares about us.

Do you remember a time when you were upset and someone just listened and said, "I understand." Didn't that make you feel a little better? That's the power of empathetic understanding. It's not as hard as you may think. For most empaths, it is in their nature. It is very natural for them to be empathetic and understanding; that is why many people are drawn to their energy and do not know why. They feel comfortable sharing their innermost thoughts and pain with empaths.

When someone is sharing his or her feelings, give the person your full attention. Listen. Really listen. Put away distractions and focus on what the person is saying. This shows him or her that you care. Ask open-ended questions: instead of asking yes-or-no questions, ask ones that encourage them to share more. For example, instead of saying, "Are you okay?" you can ask, "What's been on your mind lately?"

Remember: we all have different experiences and feelings. It's important not to criticize or judge someone for how he or she is feeling. Let the person know that his or her feelings are valid.

If you've been through something similar, it's okay to share your experience. It can help the other person see that he or she is not alone and that you understand and you won't judge the person because you have been in his or her shoes before, which is a comfort for the person, allowing him or her not to feel ashamed or embarrassed in some circumstances.

When we practise empathetic understanding, it's as if we're sending out little beams of light to brighten someone's day. It helps them heal, little by little. The person then knows he or she is not alone, and that can be very comforting.

Always remember that we all have the power to heal wounds through empathetic understanding. It's like a superpower that's inside each one of us. The more we use it, the better we can make the world around us. Next time someone is feeling down or hurt, remember these simple steps: listen, ask, don't judge, and share. You'll be amazed at the difference these things can make. We all can leave an impact on the lives of the people around us on a daily basis. Be aware, live consciously, think, and feel how you can touch the lives of those around you. Let's be the examples of understanding and kindness in the world. Together, we can heal wounds and make the world a brighter, more caring place.

## 5. Empathy for Positive Change

Through empathy, we can impact positive change. It's not about trying to save the whole world in one go; it's about creating small changes bit by bit. It's about creating a domino effect of kindness and compassion that spreads like wildfire.

We all tend to get so caught up in our busy schedules and our own lives that we forget about the struggles others might be facing. Empathy is the gentle nudge that reminds us to step into someone else's shoes and feel what that person feels. It encourages us to listen with our hearts, not just our ears.

Once I understood what it meant to be an empath and learned how to protect myself from being overwhelmed by feeling everyone else's pain and emotions and to differentiate between my feelings and those of others, I began to manage my ability to sense others' feelings, emotions, and pain, I learned to appreciate this ability as a gift, and I know that with this gift I can make a difference in the lives of the people I cross paths with.

When we truly empathize, we feel compassion. Empathy is not just about feeling sorry for someone; it's about genuinely caring and wanting to make a difference. Empathy, in its quiet yet profound way, acts as a spark for positive change. It's like a small flame that has the power to ignite a great fire of transformation.

When thinking about empathy, picture it as a key that unlocks doors to understanding and connection. Empathy isn't a grand gesture; it's found in the small moments. It's in the smile you give to a tired cashier, in the comforting words you offer to a friend in need, and in the patience you show to someone struggling. It's these little acts that ripple out, creating a positive impact that can be felt far and wide.

One of the incredible things about empathy is its ability to break down walls that people put up to protect themselves from getting hurt. It dissolves the walls that separate us and bridges the gap. When we empathize, we realize that, deep down, we all want the same things—love, understanding, and acceptance.

Empathy isn't reserved for a select few; it's a superpower we all possess. It's that voice inside us that says, "I see you, I hear you, and I'm here for you." It unites us, reminding us that we are all human and go through similar experiences. It encourages us to be supportive of each other.

In times of hardship, empathy becomes a beacon of hope. It's a glimmer of light in the darkest moments, offering comfort and solace. It's a reminder that we're not alone in our struggles and that others care and want to help.

Empathy is like a healing force, much like love. When you approach people with patience, empathy, and love, you will witness positive change in people for the better. Some who were angry or had a hard time being trustworthy started to improve when they were around me. They felt safe and not judged. They felt as if I understood them and that life could be better than they thought. Slowly, they opened up and let love in to heal their old hurts. Let's welcome empathy, care for it, and let it lead us to a nicer world, because it's in these small acts of kindness that we discover our most genuine and wonderful selves.

When we all try to understand each other and be kind regularly, it makes a difference in our close groups. This kindness can spread to the whole community and even beyond. The changes may start small, but they're still important. Even a little step forward is better than none at all.

## 6. Creating an Understanding World

Thinking back to my childhood, I recall a strong desire to care for and help others. I always wished for a world where people were kind, loving, and compassionate towards each other. I observed my parents' consistent kindness and willingness to lend a helping hand to anyone in need.

Creating a world filled with care and understanding is something I consider to be very important. In our busy lives, it's easy to forget how powerful a simple act of kindness can be. But together, we can make a big difference. There are so many ways we can spread compassion in our communities and make the world a better place for everyone.

One of the first steps towards building a more caring world is taking the time to listen and understand each other's stories. We all have unique experiences, dreams, and challenges. When we share these, we build bridges of empathy and respect. Let's be curious about each other's lives and learn from one another.

We all know that life can be tough sometimes, and we all make mistakes. It's important to remember that nobody is perfect. When someone makes a mistake, let's try to be patient and forgiving. By doing so, we create an environment where people feel safe to be themselves, to learn, and to grow.

In our neighbourhoods, there are often people who could use a helping hand. It might be a senior citizen struggling to carry groceries, or a young family in need of support. Offering help, even in small ways, shows that we care about each other's well-being. It creates a sense of belonging and strengthens the bonds in our community. I feel fortunate to have caring and helpful neighbors who are always willing to lend a hand when needed.

Smiling is powerful. Seeing your smile can make someone's day better, even if that person doesn't speak the same language as you. Let's smile more. It's free but means a lot. Words are strong. They can lift up or bring down. Let's use kind and respectful words. This makes a space of trust and openness, where everyone feels important. In the workshops I facilitate, students are encouraged to think before they speak and choose their words wisely.

We Canadians are so fortunate to be in Canada, where there are people from diverse backgrounds and diverse cultures.

For instance, I am of Chinese heritage, was born and lived in Bangladesh till the age of eight, and migrated to Pakistan and then to Canada in my late teens. I have been interacting with people from different cultures from the time I was born. Learning about each other's backgrounds and customs not only enriches our own lives but also creates a sense of unity and understanding. Accepting diversity creates a more inclusive world where everyone feels accepted and valued.

Have you ever experienced the joy of a random act of kindness? These include someone holding the door for you, or a stranger giving you a compliment. These small gestures have a big impact. They remind us that there is goodness in the world and inspire us to pass it forward. Our children are the future caretakers of this world. Let's teach them the importance of compassion and understanding. Encourage them to be kind to their friends, respectful to their elders, and accepting of those who are different from them.

Creating a more caring and understanding world is something we can all contribute to. Through simple acts of kindness, listening, and respecting one another, we can make a big difference. Let's adopt compassion in our daily lives, and together, we'll build a world where everyone feels valued, loved, and understood. Thank you for joining me on this journey towards a brighter, more caring world.

# Chapter 10

## Living an Authentic and Heartfelt Life

### 1. Loving Heart

WHEN I SPEAK OF LOVE OR A LOVING HEART, I AM NOT REFERRING to romantic love but rather love amongst friends, family, neighbours, or colleagues. Love is a selfless affection for and connection to someone or something. Love is like the special feeling we get when we connect with someone. It's what makes life feel alive and full of meaning, like a heartbeat that keeps us going.

A loving heart is filled with kindness, compassion, and warmth. It accepts and understands others without judgement. It interacts with patience and care, creating a safe space of support and trust. A loving heart is a source of positivity, a shining light to the world with its boundless affection. Love nurtures, supports, and inspires, creating bonds that endure time and challenges.

Let's talk about bringing a loving heart into our everyday lives. It's like having a warm, glowing light inside us that spreads kindness and positivity to everyone around us. No matter where we come from or what language we speak, love is a universal language that we can all understand.

Having a loving heart means being kind, caring, and considerate towards others. It's about spreading happiness, warmth, and understanding. Imagine your heart as a treasure chest filled with love, compassion, and empathy. When you have a loving heart, you share these treasures with the world.

Keeping love in my heart helps me in my work as a holistic healer when interacting with clients. They feel special and safe, which helps them in their personal and spiritual growth.

The first step in bringing a loving heart into everyday living is to be kind to yourself. This might seem a bit strange, but it's very important. Your heart is similar to a garden. You need to water and care for the flowers in a garden (which are your feelings) before you can share their beauty with others. Take a moment each day to appreciate yourself. Maybe you can do so by saying some kind words in the mirror or by doing something that makes you happy. When we treat ourselves with love, we'll find it easier to share that love with others.

Do this on a regular basis, engaging in activities that you enjoy. I love being creative and doing crafts, sewing, painting, writing, or anything that involves creativity. Getting lost in the creative process helps me tune out the world and focus on my creations, which brings me great joy when I see the end products. You, too, can indulge in activities you enjoy that make you happy.

Now let's talk about how to spread love to the people around us. We don't need grand gestures or expensive gifts. Love can be shared through small everyday acts of kindness. It's like dropping pebbles into a pond; each act creates ripples that touch others. Simple things like smiling at someone, holding the door open, or saying "thank you" can brighten someone's day. Such acts show people that you care, and it creates a chain reaction of positivity.

When we are out and about, going for walks or shopping, and we pass others, greeting them with a smile or saying hello can be very uplifting if they are going through a rough time. I have a couple of friends who are amazing and super open to greeting every single person they cross paths with. However, I am an introvert and may greet someone with a smile if our eyes meet. I am less likely to call out to them to greet them as my friends do. I am a bit more reserved and feel that some people may prefer to have their private moments, just as I do sometimes, but I would still greet someone who called out to me to say hello.

Another important way to bring love into everyday living is by listening with an open heart. When someone is talking to you, give them your full attention. Look into their eyes, nod to show you understand, and be present in that moment. This shows them that you value what they have to say. Some people may just need someone to talk to because they may not have anyone in their lives that they can get together with, especially the seniors.

When meeting people, if you come across someone who is alone or feeling lonely because he or she has no children or family, lend that person your ear and listen to his or her stories. Make the person feel that he or she is not alone. Give some of your precious time. It will bring you some satisfaction knowing you are making a difference in someone's life. Sometimes people just need someone to listen and understand them. When we do this, we're giving them a gift of love and support.

Life can be complicated, and people can be too. That's why it's important to be patient and understanding. If you were in their shoes, how would you want someone to treat you? When we approach others with patience and understanding, we're saying, "I care about you, and I'm here for you." It helps create a sense of trust and comfort, which are the foundations of any loving relationship.

Nobody's perfect. We all make mistakes. It's a part of being human. That's why forgiveness is such a powerful way to bring love into our lives. When we forgive, we release the negative feelings that can weigh us down. It's like lifting a heavy burden off our shoulders. Forgiveness doesn't mean forgetting or condoning the actions; it means letting go of the anger or resentment.

Bringing a loving heart into everyday living is a beautiful way to make the world a better place. It's like a gentle breeze that touches everyone it meets. By being kind to ourselves, spreading love through small acts of kindness, listening with an open heart, being patient and understanding, and forgiving, we create a world filled with warmth and compassion.

Remember: love is a language we can all speak, no matter where we come from. So let's embrace it, share it, and watch how it transforms our lives and the lives of those around us. Together we can make the world a brighter, more loving place.

## 2. Gratitude

What is gratitude? Gratitude is a special feeling of thankfulness. It's like saying "thank you" not just with words but with your heart. When you have gratitude, you recognize and appreciate the good things around you. It's like having a treasure chest full of happy moments.

Having an attitude of gratitude is like having a magical key that unlocks happiness in your heart. It is the warm feeling you get when you appreciate the good things in your life, big or small. In this journey of life, every moment counts, and being grateful for each one can make it even more beautiful. I would like you to explore the power of gratitude and how it can bring about a positive change in your life.

When we focus on the good things, we invite happiness into our lives. It's like having a sunbeam shining on us, warming us from the inside. Gratitude is like a soothing balm for our worries. When you look at life with a thankful heart, problems seem smaller, and stress feels lighter. When we show gratitude to others, it strengthens our bonds. It's like a glue that makes friendships and family ties even stronger.

Gratitude is like medicine for our bodies and minds. It can make us feel better, make us sleep better, and even make us more energetic. It's like putting on a pair of glasses that helps us see the bright side of things. Gratitude helps us focus on what's good even when things are tough. My clients who participate in the Healing Journey Program, learn to adopt an attitude of gratitude into their lives and soon have much more positive perspectives in life.

As you wake up, take a moment to be thankful for a new day. It's like having a fresh canvas on which to paint your life's masterpiece. Look around at the trees, flowers, and the sky. Be grateful for the beauty of the world. It's like being in a colourful painting. Enjoy the little things like a warm cup of tea, a kind smile, or a gentle breeze. These small joys are like hundreds and thousands on the cake of life. Can you imagine, if you are able to feel gratitude and happiness for even a minute thing in life, the joy and happiness you will feel when something more significant occurs?

Once I was so overjoyed over a very minor thing I got that my friend teased me about how excited I could get over something valued at a dollar's worth. She went on to say that she couldn't or wouldn't get as excited as I was if she were me. My response to her was "Can you imagine, if I can be so happy and excited over a menial thing, how much more excited I can get over something more? I will be jumping for joy."

Yes, if we are able to be grateful for everything no matter what we encounter in life, whether it be a beautiful experience or a challenging one, chances of us being unhappy are incredibly minimal or close to none. Even when things don't go as planned, there's always something to learn. Be thankful for the wisdom gained. It's like turning a stumble into a dance move.

Take a moment to appreciate the people in your life: family, friends, and even new acquaintances. They are like stars that light up your journey. Challenges can be tough, but they also make you stronger. Be grateful for the chance to grow. It's like a workout for your soul.

Write down the things you're thankful for every day. It's like collecting shiny pebbles on a beach, each one a precious memory. I know some of you may already have a gratitude journal, writing notes on the things you are grateful for every day. There are some people I know who write gratitude notes at the end of the day. I like to start and end the day with gratitude but I am grateful throughout the day. I always say a thank-you in my heart for every minute thing throughout the day.

Don't be shy about expressing your gratitude to others. It's like giving them a gift of joy. Take a deep breath and focus on what you're thankful for in that moment. It's like pressing a pause button to soak in the goodness. Even when things are tough, try to find something positive. It's like finding a silver lining in a cloudy sky.

Gratitude is a superpower that anyone can have. It's not about having everything perfect but is rather about appreciating what you have. So let's open our hearts to gratitude and watch how it transforms our lives, one thankful moment at a time. Remember: every moment is a gift, and every gift is worth being grateful for.

## 3. Being True to Yourself

I strongly believe that we all must be true to ourselves. But to be true to ourselves, we must first know more about ourselves. Who are we? What are our values, and what do we believe in? What makes us happy, and what triggers us to be upset?

Discovering and staying true to who you are is like finding a hidden treasure. It's like uncovering a map that leads to a world of freedom and happiness. In this journey, I've learned that being true to myself is the key to living a fulfilling and joyful life.

Knowing who you are, deep down inside, is like having a special compass that guides you through life's adventures. It's like recognizing the colours that make up the unique masterpiece painting that is you. Understanding your likes, dislikes, dreams, and fears helps you to navigate this world with confidence.

Embracing your true self also means accepting that you are not perfect, and that's perfectly okay. It's like understanding that every flower in a garden is beautiful, even with its unique shape and colour. Recognizing your imperfections allows you to grow and blossom in your own way. Clients are encouraged when they first start their healing journeys; they learn to accept themselves fully no matter what they think their strengths and weaknesses are. They are guided to dig deep within themselves to get to know who they are on the inside. Many of us go through life living in a way that is expected of us by others. Some go to the extent of forgetting about themselves because they are so focused on making others happy at the expense of their own happiness. Sometimes they are so used to living lives based on what is expected of them that they are unaware of why some things trigger them to be upset or what they are dealing with subconsciously from childhood experiences.

Being true to yourself gives you strength like none other. It's like wearing a suit of armour made of honesty and self-respect. When you are authentic, you can face challenges with courage, knowing that you are standing on solid ground. When you let go of trying to be someone you are not, it's like removing heavy chains that were holding you back. It's like setting a bird free to soar in the open sky. By releasing the pressure of trying to meet other people's expectations, you find true freedom.

Authenticity is like a magical key that opens the doors to meaningful relationships. It's like finding companions who appreciate you for who you are. Being true to yourself attracts people who align with your values and support your journey. You, too, will experience the same when embracing your authenticity.

Believing in taking steps towards being true to yourself is a victory. It's like collecting colourful stones on a path, each one marking a moment of growth. Whether it's a small achievement or a significant milestone, each one is a cause for celebration. We must always be willing to celebrate every achievement no matter how small, just as being grateful for everything.

A loving heart is a source of positivity, a shining light to the world with its boundless affection. Love nurtures, supports, and inspires, creating bonds that withstand time and challenges.

It's like discovering a hidden garden within yourself, full of vibrant flowers and peaceful streams. Being true to who you are sets you free from the expectations of others and allows you to live a life filled with joy, purpose, and genuine connections. Remember: you have the power to be true to yourself, and in doing so, you'll find your own path to freedom and happiness.

## 4. Expressing Your True Self

Have you ever considered how you interact with people daily? Do you hold things back for many reasons, mainly fear—fear of being judged, fear of being misunderstood, fear of hurting someone's feelings, or fear of not being liked? I can assure you that you will feel much better, in your heart, if you truly express yourself. Much of the time, these fears are unfounded.

Fear often paralyzes people, preventing them from doing many things. In my opinion, if you fear any of the above fears mentioned, there are underlying reasons. Try to determine what those fears are so you can eliminate them. People always tell me I am fearless, which is far from the truth. Like everyone else, I, too, experience fears. However, I feel that it is more important to me to be true to myself, so I choose to be my authentic self and express my thoughts or what is in my heart and let the chips fall where they may.

When someone truly values you for who you are, that person will accept what you have to say or express. He or she may not like and accept what you say, but the person will still value you and respect you for what you stand for. Expressing your true self means being genuine and authentic in how you present yourself to the world. It involves letting go of masks, pretences, and societal expectations to reveal your inner thoughts, feelings, beliefs, and desires.

Accepting yourself is about embracing your unique qualities, quirks, and strengths and allowing them to shine without fear of judgement or rejection. When you share your true self, you are being honest and transparent about who you are, both to yourself and to others. It's a powerful act of self-acceptance and a key to living a fulfilling and genuine life.

Being your true self is like turning on a light in a dark room. It's like letting your unique sparkle out into the world. I've come to learn that being authentic, being the true me, is the secret to feeling alive and connected. Finding my own voice is like discovering a powerful instrument I didn't know I had. Being raised in a culture where parents, family, and society influenced my ability to share my voice was not acceptable. It felt as if I were being held prisoner in my own home with an invisible chain and shackles.

Speaking from the heart is like realizing you have a song to sing, a story to tell. It allows you to connect with others genuinely. In my childhood years, I tried to speak my mind, only to be shut down. Letting go of cultural bondage and learning to speak up was liberating. I learned to just be me, without anyone controlling my life.

Opening up and showing our true selves, flaws and all, is like opening a window to let fresh air in. It's a bit scary at first but oh, so refreshing. Being vulnerable allows us to connect with others on a deeper level, and it helps us realize that it's okay to not have it all together. When we express our true selves, it's like discovering a secret garden of happiness. It's where we can dance to our rhythm and enjoy every step. Doing things that truly resonate with who we are brings us a special kind of joy that can't be matched.

When I let my true self shine, it's like lighting a candle in a dark room. It not only brightens my path but can also inspire others to do the same. By being authentic, you permit those around you to be themselves too. I used my own life experiences to help others to find their voices.

Life can throw curveballs, right? When you face challenges, being true to yourself is like having a sturdy boat in a stormy sea. It helps you stay grounded and make decisions that align with your values, even in the toughest times.

In the end, being your true self is like opening a beautifully wrapped gift that's been waiting for you all along. It's a journey of self-discovery, of embracing your weaknesses, your dreams, and your passions. Remember: you have a light within you that's waiting to shine. So let it out, and watch how it lights your path and the world around you.

## 5. Genuine Feelings

It was not easy being true to my feelings, because I wasn't raised to express my true feelings. In fact, when I think back, I realize I was not allowed to express my feelings, let alone my true feelings. Emotions are like a special language we all speak, no matter where we're from. They're like the heart's own words, connecting us in a way that even words can't. A smile, a tear, a laugh—they tell stories that anyone can understand, no matter what language he or she speaks.

Emotions are like a secret code that makes us all part of a big family. When we share our real feelings, we are talking to people on a basic human level. A smile or a tear can make a friendship stronger, even between friends who don't speak the same language.

Think of a time when you knew someone's feelings were true.

Maybe a friend was happy for something good that happened to you or a family member was there for you when you were sad. Those moments create trust. When we're honest with our feelings, it helps others trust us too.

Being an empath, I often sense what other people are feeling. It's also a gift that gives us the ability to be a human lie detector, so oftentimes I can sense when someone is not being honest or genuine. It is a great gift to have so we can know when we are dealing with dishonest people, yet at times it is disappointing when someone you consider to be a good friend is not being honest and you can just tell that he or she is deceiving you.

Being honest with our feelings is the glue that holds our relationships together. It lets us deeply connect with others. When we share our true feelings, it invites others to do the same. This builds trust and closeness, and it helps us understand each other better, making our relationships special.

To be real with our feelings, we have to let ourselves be seen, even when we're not perfect. This openness isn't a weakness; it's a strength. It helps us connect with others. It makes room for understanding and kindness, and it makes life richer and more real.

Understanding and accepting our feelings is super important. It helps us figure out why we think and act the way we do. This self-awareness helps us grow as people and build better, more loving relationships. Self-awareness is the most important topic I impart to my clients when I help them in their healing journeys.

Being truly honest with our feelings means not worrying about what others expect from us. It means allowing ourselves to feel deeply and share those feelings without being scared of what others might say. I prefer to be honest because I believe in painful truth rather than a kind lie. My friends are aware of this about me and appreciate it because they feel that they know where they stand with me and trust my opinions, thoughts, and suggestions because they know I will not compromise my integrity.

I feel that when we are real with our feelings, it makes us feel better overall. It helps us deal with stress, keeps our minds healthy, and makes us feel more satisfied with life. This shows just how powerful being true to our feelings can be.

In a world where people often say we should hide feelings, being honest about our emotions is like a superpower. It brings people together, builds trust, and makes our lives so much more amazing. As we embrace being real with our feelings, we are opening doors to deeper connections, becoming better people, and finding true happiness. So let's celebrate the amazing influence of being open to our feelings. They're like the heart's own language that unites us all in this big, beautiful world.

# Chapter 11

*Communication*

## 1. Forms of Communication

FROM THE TIME WE'RE BORN, WE ALL COMMUNICATE WITH EACH other every day. Even if newborn babies can't speak like grown-ups, they still know how to communicate in their own way. Babies show their feelings with their faces, how they move their bodies, and the sounds they make, such as when they cry to get the attention of their mums or dads.

All animals also communicate with each other. Every type of animal has its special way of communicating. Communicating is highly important in any type of friendship or family bond. Without communication, it's really hard to have good relationships with others.

Communication can happen in many ways. We can use words, write things down, show things with our bodies, use our eyes to show interest, use hand signs, and even, by some accounts, communicate telepathically. All these ways of communication show how much sharing and understanding mean to us, whether we're humans or animals.

## 2. Art of Communication

Communication is an important key to all relationships, whether they be business relationships or personal relationships. Personal relationships can include parent–child relationships; relationships between siblings and friends; or close relationships, such as romantic or spousal relationships.

How we communicate with others is important, as it is what can either break a relationship or create strong bonds with others.

We need to learn the art of communication so we can have good, genuine relationships with each other. Being mindful of how we speak to others, choosing words that will not offend or hurt others, and being careful of how we use our tone when we speak are all arts of communication. All of this helps prevent miscommunication. When I speak of the art of communicating, I am not referring to being dishonest, although some people who have skills in the art of communication are very successful in pulling scams.

I encourage you to master the art of communication to help you with your relationships with the people you encounter in your daily life. Having the ability to communicate well encourages happy and harmonious relationships. Most importantly, your communication must be honest and from your heart.

Communicating mindfully with your loved ones can significantly enhance your relationships and bring you closer. It means being present, listening actively, and showing kindness. Avoid interruptions, stay open-minded, and be patient. Express gratitude, apologize, and forgive when needed. Practicing mindful communication makes you better at it, and the result is stronger, more meaningful relationships.

# 3. Boundaries in Communications:

In communication, it is advisable to set healthy boundaries for healthy and respectful interaction with others. Boundaries are those invisible lines that are acceptable and comfortable for you. They are crucial for maintaining positive relationships, managing conflicts, and ensuring your well-being.

To establish effective boundaries, we must first be aware of our own needs, values, and limits. Reflect on what makes you comfortable or uncomfortable in various communication scenarios.

Communicate clearly what your boundaries are to others. Use "I" statements to express your feelings and needs without blaming or accusing others. For example, say, "I need some alone time right now" instead of "You're always bothering me." When we allow ourselves to be open to personal growth and be the best versions of ourselves, our perceptions change and we learn to communicate better. What we hear also changes.

Just as we have boundaries, others have them too. Respect their boundaries as you would want them to respect yours. This creates a reciprocal atmosphere of mutual respect. When someone tells you that he or she needs some alone time, respect that person's boundaries just as you do when you want your space. When you feel you want to communicate your feelings to your spouse or loved one but are not in the mood to engage in deep communication, do not insist on it, as it will not have the results you hoped for and may lead to conflict, which can lead to misunderstanding. It's crucial to be mindful of our loved ones and those we wish to communicate with, whether or not they are receptive to what it is we wish to say.

It is also best to have consistency in maintaining boundaries. If we enforce our boundaries sporadically, others may not take them seriously. We will appear to be indecisive. Be firm but respectful in upholding your limits. However, there should also be room for flexibility and compromise in certain situations. Not all circumstances are the same, and sometimes you might need to adjust your boundaries to accommodate others.

Setting boundaries is a form of self-care. It's about prioritizing your mental, emotional, and physical health. Recognize that it's okay to say no or to step away from a conversation or situation that is causing you stress or discomfort. Boundaries can help prevent conflicts by clarifying expectations. However, when conflicts do arise, use effective communication skills to address them constructively. Seek compromise and understanding rather than confrontation.

In a professional setting, it's crucial to maintain appropriate boundaries with colleagues, clients, and superiors. This helps create a respectful and ethical work environment. Boundaries in communication are a vital component of healthy and respectful relationships, both personal and professional. They empower individuals to express their needs and limits while respecting the autonomy and boundaries of others. By practising clear communication and consistently enforcing your boundaries, you can create a more harmonious and fulfilling communication environment.

## 4. Heartfelt Communication

Consider having a heart-to-heart conversation with the person you are communicating with. When we engage in such conversations, we can achieve several positive outcomes. We will gain better understandings of each other's perspectives, feelings, and experiences, which can strengthen our relationships and build trust. Deepen emotional bonds between people, whether it's between friends, family members, romantic partners, or even colleagues. This can create a sense of closeness and mutual support. It's also a way to find emotional relief, resolve problems, and improve your communication skills. Plus you might even deepen your emotional bond and experience personal growth. So why not take the opportunity to connect on a deeper level and address any issues or concerns you may have? It could lead to a more meaningful and fulfilling connection.

Engaging in heart-to-heart conversations can strengthen relationships by building trust and emotional intimacy. It can help resolve conflicts and address issues that may have been causing tension. It can also help individuals develop better communication skills, including active listening, empathy, and emotional intelligence. Heart-to-heart communication can be a productive way to address problems and find solutions. It can lead to constructive problem-solving and compromise. It deepens emotional bonds between people, whether between friends, family members, romantic partners, or even colleagues. It can create a sense of closeness and mutual support.

It's important to note that the specific results of heart-to-heart communication can vary widely depending on the individuals and circumstances involved. Not all heart-to-heart conversations will lead to positive outcomes, as emotions and interpersonal dynamics can be complex. However, when approached with sincerity and empathy, heart-to-heart communication can be a valuable tool for building connections and resolving emotional issues.

I like to encourage my friends, clients, and students to communicate with others while holding love in their hearts, as doing so can be incredibly helpful. When we approach conversations with a loving attitude, we create an environment of warmth, understanding, and compassion. Our words and actions become more genuine and considerate, creating positive connections with those around us.

This loving approach can lead to improved relationships, as it promotes trust and empathy. It helps us navigate conflicts better, as we're then more likely to seek resolution and compromise instead of confrontation. Ultimately, communicating with love in our hearts not only benefits our interactions with others but also contributes to a more harmonious and loving world. My hope is for the world to be more loving and kinder all around. If each of us makes the effort to be loving and kind, there will be more love among each other.

## 5. Sharing What's in Our Hearts

Talking and communicating are things humans do to connect with others. We talk about everyday things, but there are some things that are more important, such as telling others what's really in our hearts. This means sharing our true feelings, thoughts, and wishes. This helps us connect better with people, grow personally, and build strong relationships.

When we speak about what's in our hearts, we show our true selves to others. This can help create deeper, more honest friendships. Sharing our joys, fears, hopes, and even our worries allows people to know the real us. This openness often makes others trust and care for us more because we are being more authentic when we do.

Holding in our feelings can be unhealthy for our mental and emotional well-being. Talking about how we feel is like releasing pressure from a bottle. It can make us feel better, reduce our stress, and help us find comfort in the support of others who care for us.

When we honestly talk about our feelings, it helps resolve problems. Keeping emotions hidden during disagreements can cause misunderstandings and anger. Eventually it can lead to angry outbursts, which can ultimately cause conflicts in relationships. Speaking from the heart allows us to express ourselves, understand others, and find solutions that make everyone happy. It is also important to speak when we are calm and rational.

Sharing our feelings helps us understand ourselves better. When we talk about our thoughts and emotions, it's like looking in a mirror. This self-awareness can help us become better people by identifying areas where we can improve and live in line with our values. It encourages others to empathize with us. They can then better understand what we are going through. Empathy is crucial for strong relationships and making the world a better place.

Strong relationships often start with open, heartfelt conversations. Sharing our thoughts and emotions brings people closer, whether they're friends, family, or partners. It helps create a warm and caring environment. Openly sharing our experiences and concerns can inspire others to do the same. This builds communities where people support each other and work together for positive change.

Sharing what's in our hearts isn't just about feeling better. It's essential for connecting with others, resolving conflicts, growing personally, and making the world a kinder place. It's a part of being human that lets us share our joys, fears, hopes, and worries. In a world that sometimes talks about only surface-level things, we should recognize how valuable it is to speak from the heart to enrich our lives and the lives of others.

# Krista's Journey

Krista is a client who started her healing Journey when she was going through emotional turmoil during her marital separation with her ex-husband. When I introduced the Healing Journey to her and explained how the healing could help calm her emotions and help her to deal with the challenges she was going through and transition through her marital separation with a calm and clear mind, which would benefit not only her but her family as well, she was open to what the Healing Journey offered.

As she started her Healing Journey, she felt a sense of peace and focus and found that the ability to be calm from the healing helped her deal with the emotional roller coaster without feeling angry. I have my clients write self-assessments on how they are doing and what they have accomplished from their commitment to their personal growth. Krista has given me permission to share her self-assessment in order to share her story regarding how the Healing Journey Program helped her with her personal and spiritual growth.

**Krista's Self-Assessment Based on Her Healing Journey Session:**

> When I think back to how it began and reflect on what I was going through at the time of its conception, I am filled with emotions of anxiety and nervousness in my stomach. My body is hot

171

with emotions. I know now that I am capable of harnessing these emotions from running wild in my mind. Tame them to feel them, acknowledge them, and then let them go. So here it goes. Taking a deep breath, I dive in.

My life encountered a turning point when my father in law passed away in 2012. This loss was deep for Charles and I. We handled it differently. I was emotional. It created a lot of anxiety within me. I didn't know how to release it in a healthy way so it stayed within and amplified. Charles was stoic and disconnected. I know now that is how he deals with his emotions but at the time, I didn't realize this and misunderstood his reactions and how he was with me. I feel that is when we started to drift apart. In time, the gap between us grew as we perceived each other as being unsupportive.

For years after, anxiety would emerge, I became defensive, put my head down and soldered forward. I encountered anxiety attacks. I was depressed for a time. Felt alone, cried and always felt tired. I created this mind state of overwhelm and fear of life moving too fast and having too many responsibilities. I was no longer enjoying life. Weighted down by family, relationships and work responsibilities, I lost myself. I didn't make time to care for myself and as a result I became resentful and bitter towards Charles as I felt unsupported. So my life became unsettled, exhausting and heavy. I felt that I was always treading water to maintain a sense of calm. It was not sustainable. All I wanted was to rest on solid and stable ground but I constantly had to shift to help others and meet expectations.

Then, our marriage encountered a crisis. I was knocked off my feet. I fell down and shattered into pieces. I was broken and emotionally, mentally and physically ill. Wow, when I reflect, I see that I was a mess at this time. All broken down by the emotional and mental stress. In my time of need, I was guided to a divorce coach that encouraged emotional discovery work and identifying feelings to move one through the stress of a marital separation. My focus was redirected to things that made me happy, lifted me up and made me feel light. It was my first aha moment of how my emotions were controlling my thought patterns and affecting me and others around me.

Then, I met Jacinta and my world of greater possibilities opened up. She opened the door, held my hand, walked me through to the other side. The healing journey began. Though I did not know it at the time, I felt the pull to go with her and delighted in the joy and lightness she radiated when I attended her reiki sessions. Over time, she compassionately worked on stabilizing my emotional state and guided me towards methods to practice for elevating my well being. My world became brighter, there was renewed hope, I was laughing again and untangling my thoughts and emotions. I was learning new ways of thinking. Opened up to a new world of energy and crystal healing. Explored the benefits of listening to my intuition and supporting my inner soul health through practices of spirituality and meditation. I felt the transition to slowing my world down and becoming aware of the moment and the beauty that is within nature and spiritually with us everyday. I was feeling and seeing the benefits. I am moving away from the fog of entanglement and thinking clearer with a purpose. I learned to release resentment, tame anger, be more compassionate and less judgemental of others. I work on empathy, compassion and acceptance. Most of all I work on self-love, self care. The brain is pliable. I realize now that I have the power in me to change my thinking and to reframe it. I dived into personal work and realized that progression is through personal and spiritual growth. I identified things that were not working for me and ways to improve it. My communication approach needed a lot of work. The act of putting my head down and soldering through proved not to be the way to move forward. I began shifting my communication approach with my children, with Charles and with my other relations. Opening up, saying how I felt, being clear on my intentions. It hurt alot. I cried many times and felt terrible because this went against my beliefs of creating ease. I felt as though I was not going with the flow. What I learned though, is that it is painful at first when it is all out on the table. It is like a closet when you attempt to clean it up. All of it comes out of the closet. You look around and see the enormity of the pile of stuff removed. You go through a rediscovery of all the stuff you have thrown into the closet over the years. Some you forgot about, some items are so old that you wonder why you kept it for so long and some you see that it is useful and needs to stay. This decluttering of my life was essential for my progress. I trust that what I have endured is preparing me for a greater task ahead. I am open to the possibilities. I delight in the journey ahead. I know that I will be presented with barriers and sometimes get lost but I am confident now that I may just stop and ask for help and remain open to receiving the signs to direct me. I trust that when I follow my instincts and align it with my beliefs that I will feel right in my soul and will travel the path I am meant to be on. I aspire to be that source of light for others to find their way too. Like Jacinta was to me and how she has shared her knowledge, shown compassion, love, empathy and understanding, I will maintain these qualities into my everyday encounters.

Thank you for taking me under your wing. The journey continues and it is a wondrous and glorious view!

At Jacinta Healing Arts, we are honored to accompany you on your journey towards holistic well-being and self-discovery. If you're ready to embark on your own transformative journey, we invite you to take the first step today. Your story awaits.

Printed in the United States
by Baker & Taylor Publisher Services